TONY MOON

ROOFTOP KOREAN

옥상시민군 사이구

A MEMOIR OF THE 1992 L.A. RIOTS

Version 1.0, First Printing

Published by WarGate Books, Puyallup, WA

Printed in the United States of America

EBOOK ISBN: 979-8-88922-158-6
HARDCOVER ISBN: 979-8-88922-137-1
Library of Congress Control Number: 2026944266

All photographs are from the author's collection, unless otherwise noted

Cover Design: M.S. Corley
Website:WarGatebooks.com

DEDICATION

To my Loveys,

God's plan for you is greater than any plan you can imagine for yourself.

—Dada

A NOTE FROM THE AUTHOR

This book is a work of nonfiction. The events described are true and are drawn from my own memory, along with conversations with the friends and family who lived them alongside me.

That said, I want to be honest with you about a few things before we begin.

Many of these events took place more than thirty years ago. The dialogue in these pages is not a transcript — it's my best recollection of what was said, reconstructed to capture the truth and spirit of those conversations as I remember them. If you were there too and remember a word or two differently, I don't doubt you. Memory is its own kind of storyteller.

I've changed some names. A few of the people in this book have built lives far from the ones described here, and they didn't ask to have their pasts printed on a page and placed in a stranger's hands. Others I simply wanted to protect. Where I've used a changed name, I've still tried to tell their story faithfully and with respect, because these are people I cared about, and in many cases, still do.

Finally, the opinions in this book are mine alone. When I write about the things I lived through and the conclusions I've drawn from them, I'm telling you how I see it, not handing you a verdict. You're free to weigh it all for yourself. In fact, I hope you do.

With that, let's begin.

— Tony Moon

Jesus replied, "Very truly I tell you, no one can see the Kingdom of God unless you are born again."

—John 3:3

INTRODUCTION

It was the first time I used a metal water bottle as a weapon. The 22-ounce bottle was almost empty, making a uniquely light *thunk* when it connected with the person's head.

The date was July 3, 2021, in Koreatown, Los Angeles, during a protest against allowing men to pretend to be women in the women's section of a Korean spa called Wi Spa.

One of the counter-protesters made the mistake of coming at me physically, assuming there would be no consequence. It had been a long time since I had hit someone over the head with anything, but the movement was instinctual, coming naturally without much thought, from years of turning anything in my hand into a weapon. It brought me back to the time when

I was much younger, a teen growing up in Los Angeles during the mid-1980s and early '90s.

When the counter-protester came at me the second time, I had to make sure the self-proclaimed "journalists" working together to set me up by distracting me with asinine questions —such as "Why are you wearing a Roof Korean T-shirt?" and "Don't you know it's racist?"—weren't going to sucker-punch me. With the second hit, I heard one of them yell, "Oh shit!"

Oh shit is right, idiots. You confronted the wrong person today, flashed through my mind. I knocked aside the counter-protester's arms and gave a second clean hit with the metal water bottle.

"Yo, yo, yo, man, what the fuck!" one of the "journalists" shouted. I guess the situation wasn't going in the direction they'd anticipated.

I had been through enough confrontations as a teenager in L.A. to see through their setup: preoccupy/distract with stupid comments and questions, while the "enforcer" of dubious gender runs up and goes for a groin kick.

I've started and been involved in enough fights to know how the fight game is played on the streets.

The LAPD officers approached—they had been standing just fifteen feet away—and the "journalists" tried to pin me as the instigator, attacking without provocation. What a bunch of idiots.

An officer who had seen everything stepped in and asked me to put down the water bottle. I readily complied, although I had previously ignored the whining "journalist" attempting to order me to do the same. "Put that shit down!" the "journalist" had commanded, as if I were the aggressor, and then as soon as LAPD stepped in, it became, "Can you please ask him to put it down?"

I found out who he was months later: one of many leftist "journalists" looking for content to skew and fit a narrative to post online.

The officer escorted me away, saying, "I'm just going to walk you to the other side," and then released me. Dealing with LAPD was a familiar feeling, taking me back to a time in the distant past—a time when a much younger me was living a completely different life…

PART ONE: GROWING UP KOREAN IN L.A.

CHAPTER ONE

Fourteen was not a good age for me. That year, 1986, was the year my mother died of leukemia.

It was also the year I was recruited into gang life—a life that would thrust me into the violent center of the 1992 L.A. Riots.

Prior to her death, my mother had been the connector between me and my father—the communicator—and her passing greatly impacted our relationship. My father hardly ever spoke to me, and when he did, it was to criticize. I never did things the way he wanted, or put in the amount of effort he expected. He reminded me—regularly—of my perceived shortcomings. I tried to please him, but even when I was accepted into a highly gifted program at seven years old, the best I received was a nod of approval and a solemn "You did good" in Korean.

I was in awe of my father, and afraid of him. Standing at over six feet tall, he had a slim and athletic build, with a rectangular face and square-rimmed glasses. His stern gaze had the ability to snap me back out of whatever daydream or thought I had and directly into the moment. And if that gaze turned to one of anger, I wanted to crawl into myself and disappear.

When my mother passed away, our relationship deteriorated. My father started drinking heavily, but only at home. He put up a good front at the market he owned in Huntington Park. Eventually, though, he began drinking earlier and earlier in the day. This was a wake-up call that spurred him to stop drinking. I overheard him telling my uncles and my grandfather (my mother's father) that he intended to quit because of how bad it had gotten.

At that point in my life, though, what my father was going through didn't mean much to me. I was in and out of the house, avoiding him as much as I could, sleeping at friends' houses, or other various places in the neighborhood—apartment laundry rooms, the alley behind Pier 1 Imports, the roof of the school across the street. I had become one of the youngest members in an established and notorious Filipino L.A. gang called Bahala Na Gang (meaning the "I-don't-care gang"; "Bahala Na" was an expression of "whatever" in Tagalog, the main language of the Philippines), or just BNG. We used a question mark as our symbol, in keeping with our unpredictability.

Looking back, I realized I pushed my father to the end of his patience and sanity. At one point, we physically fought during an argument. The fight ended with me holding him down in a headlock as we screamed at each other. It was a sad and difficult time for both of us, but at the time, I could only see my own grief and problems.

My father was hurting and broken as well. After my mother's funeral, we had gathered at my uncle's house. My father had been drinking through his pain. He drunkenly cursed God.

"There is no God," he said. "God damn you!"

He threw away his faith that day, and I don't know if he ever found it again, because he never went to a church between then and his sudden passing in 2005.

Prior to then, we had both attended a Korean church, and even given money for their ministry, asking for a miracle for my mother. Going to church used to be a regular thing when I was younger, before my father purchased the market in Boyle Heights and my mother gave up her ambition to become a registered nurse. Life became busy and we attended more sporadically; going to church was, for us, more about partaking in a social gathering for Koreans than an act of faith.

And when those prayers to save my mother weren't answered, not even the social gathering was enough to bring my father back.

BNG looked at God like it looked at everything else… a big question mark. Whatever. But I didn't agree with my father's statement. I knew there was a God. I just felt He was too busy, and we were too insignificant for Him to care.

CHAPTER TWO

At fourteen, I was already 160 pounds and muscular, or else I'd have never gotten my father into a headlock. I knew how to fight, having had my share of street training along the way. In the L.A. of that time, fights involving large groups were common. Gangs confronted rivals, often with baseball bats, chains, sticks, nunchakus, and knives. The Filipinos had their own open-hand fight style and weaponry, which included butterfly knives and a stick-and-knife fighting style called *escrima*. But the weapon that caught my interest was the *pana*—a slingshot made from a bike tire inner tube, combined with a dart made from a nail, with feathers (or strips from a plastic bag) tied at the end. When I was a boy, I used marbles and small stones with a slingshot, so the pana felt familiar. It was a common weapon used by gangs in the Philippines because it was cheap and silent, unlike a firearm. It was also easy to conceal and easy to dispose of—you could quickly take it apart and make the pieces look unrelated.

In addition to the school of the streets, I also had formal training in combat Tae Kwon Do. In 1979, when I was seven, my father signed me up at Hollywood Tae Kwon Do, across the street from KTLA Studios on Sunset Boulevard and Bronson Avenue. My instructor, Master Kim, was part of the new wave of martial artists from South Korea coming to America. Many chose to settle in Los Angeles because of Hollywood and the opportunity to do stunt work in the movie industry. In the late 1970s and 1980s, interest had exploded in Tae Kwon Do, which propelled movies like *Best of the Best*. What a memorable movie—it told a great story of friendship, redemption, and honor.

I joined the studio in time to participate in the Hollywood premiere of Bruce Lee's last movie, *Game of Death*. That's the one where he died before the movie finished filming, so it's heavily edited and uses a number of stand-in body doubles. Many of the martial arts schools from varying disciplines showed up that opening night, and Lee's widow, Linda, gave a speech. It felt almost like an unofficial martial arts convention, with different disciplines wearing their specific type of clothing and holding banners with their school names. I loved it and I knew whatever I was a part of that night was something I wanted to belong to for the rest of my life.

Master Kim was very entrepreneurial; he networked with his Tae Kwon Do friends and contacts in Hollywood enough so that for a brief period of time, Drew Barrymore attended our school. This was after the movie *E.T.* was released, and everyone knew who she was. One day, I was to demonstrate a move in front of her with some other, less famous kid. I was nervous because my nose was running that day and I didn't want to make a bad impression on Drew.

My master wanted me to finish my demonstration with a spinning back kick, and I was a nervous wreck. My main concern was not the move, but the extremely high odds of my snot flying from my nose and splattering Drew Barrymore. I performed as instructed, and all of my bodily fluids stayed inside. My snot was not the reason she left after a couple of weeks and never returned.

Master Kim had other ways of making money with his studio that went beyond local star power. He also retailed martial arts supplies and weaponry at his school. A corner section of his studio had large glass panels facing the sidewalk in full view of pedestrian traffic, and he had an impressive full display: real katanas, staffs, batons, nunchakus, and—the favorite for us kids—a variety of throwing stars.

There was a short alley behind the studio, and Master Kim would prop up a couple of wooden pallets on the concrete wall, so we could throw. (This was before California deemed throwing stars illegal.) It was the thing to do after our class ended and before the adult class started. Sometimes even the adults, generally guys in their mid to late twenties and early thirties, would join us. The pallets stayed up until someone complained—probably a mom driving through the alley to pick up her son and thought what we were doing was too dangerous.

There was a mix of kids in my class—Mexicans, Armenians, Koreans, whites, and blacks—but the majority were Armenians or Koreans. Most of the Armenians in Hollywood were actually from Russia—Russian-Armenians—and they had a reputation of being ruthless and tough that made their brethren from Iran or Armenia-proper speak of them with respect and fear. At an urban junior high school on Bronson Avenue between Sunset and Santa Monica Boulevard called Le Conte Junior High, a small group of Armenians banded together calling themselves “AP,” for “Armenian Power,” and later on, they would develop into a full-fledged street gang that fought against the Hispanic gangs, with some members moving beyond to become a criminal syndicate with ties to the Russian Mafia.

Many of us grew up together, attending the same junior high or elementary schools. One week, there was a huge brawl between the Korean and Armenian boys at Le Conte Junior

High School, and it carried over to the Tae Kwon Do studio. Master Kim had to bring the boys into his office to talk with them. That settled things down in junior high for a while, but the mix of gangs and allegiances continued at Hollywood High.

During lunch, the quad was full of guys from different gangs, or “crews,” hanging out around the snack shop, checking in on the other crews, sharing information, and negotiating deals. Almost everyone was doing something sketchy. One semester, about half of the JROTC (Junior Reserve Officer Training Corps), a school program designed for young men and women to teach discipline, character, and service with some going into the military after graduating, was arrested for selling weed. Everyone had already known they were “dealing,” and some remarked that it was only a matter of time before they were caught, since they were so blatant about it. The guy who ran it all was a senior, and was arrested during an intermission before lunch; as he was walking out, he gave a head nod to those watching and remarked, “I’ll be back.” All I could do was nod in return. I knew he wouldn’t be back; they had too much on him.

Despite all the different crews, we were from the same neighborhood and knew one another. It wasn’t uncommon to find me hanging out with Asians, Armenians, Hispanics, and blacks. I was laughing and joking with Sons of Samoa (islanders from Samoa that are under the Crips umbrella), Armenian Power, White Fence (one of the oldest Mexican-American gangs in Los Angeles) and Hoover Crips.

Gangs kept LAPD really busy in the mid-to-late '80s and '90s, enough so that the police formed a special unit called CRASH (Community Resources Against Street Hoodlums) to combat them. They went after everyone. There weren't many white gangs in L.A., but we Asians were special enough that we had a unit all to ourselves within the LAPD called the Asian Task Force. Asian gangs were both different and similar to Hispanic gangs in that period, depending on how you grew up. Some members were from middle-income or affluent families, and wore baggy pants, loose T-shirts or button-up shirts, and espadrille-type shoes (a canvas slip-on loafer type of footwear). Those who grew up in Hispanic neighborhoods or were from lower-income areas took on the wardrobe style of the Hispanic gangs: the plain white crewneck T-shirt with a super starched and ironed crease down the middle, oversized Levi's 501 blue jeans starched and creased to the point that some guys would almost make them stand on their own when they went to bed… and the shoes had to be white Nike Cortez.

That was how Eddie Lee was dressed on Friday, May 1, 1992, when he was shot and killed by accident. But none of that had happened yet.

Hollywood High in the mid-to-late '80s was dominated by gangs. Football games between rival schools meant a fight, and a possible stabbing or shooting, after the game. There were no mass school shootings back then. How could there be when so many students were armed? There were no metal detectors, and anyone could carry anything they wanted onto campus. Ironic to consider that in the era of drive-by shootings and freeway shootings, there weren't mass school shootings.

There's a saying that an armed society is a polite society. School was our shared armed society, representing our neighborhood. Despite being in different crews, an unspoken truce developed from our friendships at school. If an out-of-neighborhood rival of *any* gang came on campus or showed up at one of the usual hangouts—such as Tony's hamburger shack across the street from school—everyone would join the brawl, backing up the guys from our neighborhood no matter what crew they were with.

Some say that racism was more prevalent back in those days, and that's probably true to a certain extent. It was certainly more out in the open. But when it came to the gangs, we only saw which neighborhood someone was from, regardless of race.

CHAPTER THREE

On Hollywood Boulevard, east of Wilton Avenue, there was a small mom-and-pop Armenian-owned liquor store that allowed you to buy beer as a minor by simply bringing a note from your parent (usually the father) asking the store owner to "allow my son to buy beer" (it was the sons who bought the beer for their fathers). As wild as that sounds, it was fairly common in the '70s and '80s.

When my father owned his market in Boyle Heights, a largely Hispanic-populated city east of downtown L.A., ten-year-old kids, or even younger, would come in with a note, and we'd sell them a six-pack of Budweiser, or a thirty-two-ounce big bottle of (usually) Miller High Life, a popular brand at that time. Of course, that practice made it trivially easy for minors to acquire alcohol.

I took advantage of this custom one day at the Armenian liquor store. I went in with a "note from my father" requesting three thirty-two-ounce bottles of Miller High Life. One was for me, and two were for the older kids I hung out with. Both were sixteen, were already drinking on occasion, and they were looking forward to seeing me get drunk with them for the first time.

We finished our beers and rode the 181 bus line on Hollywood Boulevard from Wilton to Highland Avenue near the Mann Chinese Theater. I don't remember much of the ride, with one exception: when the bus made the left turn on Highland Avenue from Hollywood Boulevard, all thirty-two ounces gushed out of my mouth and nose, spilling into the middle aisle where I was sitting, which was the very last row of seats at the back of the bus. It didn't help that Highland Avenue was on a downward incline and we were facing downward, so when the bus stopped, all the beer rolled toward the front of the bus like a flash flood.

I was disgusted and amazed, stifling a laugh while my friends, Tim and Patrick, helped me stagger off the bus through the back exit. The bus driver yelled, "Who's going to clean this up?" and Patrick shot back, "You are!"

Patrick was Thai, with a smart mouth. He was good at quick comebacks that made you laugh—unless you were on the receiving end. His parents had a large craftsman house in Hollywood just north of Hollywood Boulevard before Franklin Avenue, and they had a few arcade games in the garage, the ones that have a slot to feed quarters. Patrick's parents had a business that placed these games in certain locations, like liquor stores, markets, and bowling alleys.

Patrick's older brother was a senior member in a gang called Oriental Boys, or OB. After some time, the younger guys changed the name to LAOB, for Los Angeles Oriental Boys. Some of the younger OB would mess with Patrick when he went to Hollywood High because he wore thick Coke-bottle glasses, had a crooked front tooth, and had ears that kind of stuck out until he grew his hair long enough to cover them. But when his older brother showed up to school, all of that stopped; they'd had no idea Patrick was related to one of their main guys. How could they? The pair looked nothing alike. Patrick's big brother was tall and had a smooth calmness and charisma that made the younger guys look up to him. In contrast, Patrick looked like the hunchback of Notre Dame with glasses; he even walked like he had a hunch sometimes. There was also a strange vibe about him because he always wanted to prove himself, and as a result, he did the dumbest things.

One evening when I was with him, he was fidgeting with his BB gun. He turned to me and said, "I'm faster than my BB gun." He claimed he could fire it at his hand and move his hand out of the way faster than the BB could travel through the barrel.

Say what?

At first, I thought he was bluffing, or just talking crap as a joke. My only reply was "What? How?"

But Patrick was serious. He was going to do it.

He ended up shooting his hand, of course. The BB lodged itself between his middle and ring fingers. He was shocked at the amount of blood running down his hand, and I was struck speechless, having witnessed one of the dumbest things in my life up to that point. Eventually, after staring at all that blood for a while, he got up, mumbling something about telling his mom and that I should leave.

Yeah, he told his mom all right. Patrick must've put part of the blame on me for that incident even though he swore that he didn't. There was a No Trespassing sign on the gate in their driveway, and after the incident, Patrick's mom added "especially Tony Moon" with a black marker. The sign was also moved from the gate, which was halfway up their driveway, to his father's truck, parked at the entrance of the driveway, taped to the rear window—so everyone walking on the sidewalk could read it and know that this Tony Moon guy wasn't welcome.

That was the last time I met with Patrick at his house. We were already drifting apart because we were being recruited by two different gangs. His mom banishing me accelerated things.

A few years later, I heard that the BB was still lodged in his hand. It wasn't removed because it sat too close to a nerve and the doctor didn't want to risk cutting or damaging it. What an idiot.

My other drinking buddy that day was Tim, who was Egyptian. Only in a big city like L.A. could you make friends with an Egyptian as a kid. We'd meet at his apartment, and often his dad would be just outside the front door, telling Tim to get his act together. Tim would always retort with "I know, I know…" mixed in with some Egyptian. Then there would be a bit of back-and-forth with his dad before Tim would finally say, "Stop, my friends are here now!" His dad, with a thick Egyptian accent and slightly broken English, would come back with something like, "I don't give a shit about your friend thinking," and Patrick and I would smirk while watching their interaction. Sometimes Patrick and I would later talk to Tim like his father, imitating his accent: "Tim, where are you going with your life? When are you going to admit that you are gay loser?"

Even though they were sixteen and I was fourteen, all three of us had a knack for finding trouble, and we spent our days doing things that had us chased by LAPD.

I remember the day when we entered an old, abandoned five-story red brick apartment complex that was due to be demolished to build newer apartments. We ran and yelled between the floors, loud enough for the neighbors in the adjacent apartment buildings to call the cops. Four squad cars and eight officers surrounded the building, with more showing up. At first, we hid in the building, then Tim and I snuck out and stood with the other bystanders.

Patrick was still inside, hiding in a boiler or a furnace. He told us later how he crawled into a space and closed a small metal door behind him, then listened to the officers walk around looking for us. Meanwhile, Tim and I were outside with some of the other kids from the neighborhood, trying to get the heat off of us. We told the officers in charge of crowd control that we thought it was a gang called TPT (not a real gang—it was just the initials from our first names!), a rough bunch of guys that was making trouble in the neighborhood. The officers scribbled it all down on their little notepads, looking up periodically to ask a follow-up question that we'd answer while looking serious, with a tinge of fear for emphasis. The other kids in the neighborhood asked who TPT was, and when we told them, they started laughing with us.

No one went to jail that night. The cops finally left and Patrick came out to rejoin the TPT crew. But we would have plenty of other close calls.

Some nights, we'd scale the wall at Hollywood Forever Cemetery (this was before they installed the barbed wire) to drink wine coolers (we were kids and they tasted almost like soda) or beer, and spook ourselves with ghost stories then dare each other to run through the cemetery.

When LAPD officers showed up, we'd first hide in the darkness of the cemetery. Once they were on the other side of the place, we would spring up from our hiding spots and run to scale the wall and flee across Santa Monica Boulevard, through the adjacent neighborhoods.

I distinctly remember running on top of the cinderblock walls that divided the homes, and the four German shepherds at one house would leap high, trying to bite our shoes and pull us down. If it wasn't cinderblock walls, then it was scaling chain-link fences while making our way to residential or commercial rooftops, then dropping into an alley and running through to another block before repeating a variation of what we did before.

I suppose someone gave running from the cops a name and called it *parkour*.

At fourteen, I did a lot of parkour.

CHAPTER FOUR

The friendship between Tim, Patrick, and me lasted for over a year and a half before we drifted toward other friends. During that time, we rode the bus throughout Hollywood and Santa Monica, going to and from different parts of the city. And during the summer, to the beach.

Riding the bus to the beach from Santa Monica Boulevard meant taking the 420 bus line—back when the bus company was known as RTD (Rapid Transit District)—from Santa Monica Boulevard on Western Avenue going west until we ended up near the Santa Monica Pier. It meant riding through an area of gays and transvestites. These rides were usually uneventful.

Except this one time…

On this particular bus ride, coming back from the beach, we were joined by Thomas, one of Patrick's friends. Thomas was half Mexican and half white, and lived near Santa Monica

Boulevard and Vine Street. He was a cool guy, part of a crew called the Mid City Stoners, guys who listened to rock, smoked weed, and fought against other “stoner” gangs in Hollywood. Despite being a member of a stoner gang, he never got high on marijuana; he preferred to drink instead.

Thomas was clean-cut and liked wearing dark blue jeans and a black T-shirt with a pocket for his cigarettes. He was older than me by over two years and would look out for me when we were all out together, even though I was almost as big as he was. Like many of us, he had problems at home, too. His mom worked long hours, leaving Thomas, his younger sister and his older brother alone. I don’t know how much older his brother was, but I knew he was in a wheelchair from an accident. I also knew that the guy liked drinking, and that one time he got drunk and tried to molest their sister, who was fifteen at the time. Thomas found out, confronted his brother, and punched him in the face, knocking him out of the wheelchair while his sister was crying in her room.

Thomas told me and Patrick all of this calmly and nonchalantly on the day it happened, when we met up with him outside his house. Our eyes were wide and our mouths hung slightly open, while he smoked a cigarette.

Then his older brother wheeled himself out and said, “Don’t stay out too long.”

To which Thomas responded, "You're not our dad, and don't do that shit again."

"I was drunk. It wasn't me."

"Whatever. Let's go, guys…"

We didn't bring it up again that night or anytime afterward. We probably would've never known about it if we hadn't been there to pick him up that evening and he felt like talking. The majority of the time with Thomas, he just had that crooked smile and would say things that made us laugh.

It took us an hour and a half on the bus to get to the beach. We walked the pier, and only got into the water up to our ankles. None of us brought shorts, and we weren't planning on swimming. On the ride back home, we took our usual seats. We always took the corner spots of the last row, which stretched all the way across and wasn't separated by an aisle. When those seats weren't available, we sat close to the rear exit, in the seat that faced the side of the bus instead of being forward-facing, since it meant our backs were against a window and not another row of seats behind us. On this trip, I was in a back corner, and we fell asleep.

We woke up about twenty minutes from our stop and found four gay guys sitting next to us and around us. How did I know they were gay? I'm a light sleeper on the bus, and during the ride, I could hear the conversation between the guys, and they were definitely the flamboyant type—loud, expressive, and over the top with their personalities. If you've been around a few, you know what I mean. The ones sitting next to Tim and Patrick were purposely brushing their thighs against them and giving each other furtive glances while smiling, knowing exactly what they were doing, even though we were minors. Then the guy who sat next to Patrick draped his arm over the back of Patrick's seat, making Patrick and him look like a couple. Luckily for me, no one could try that trick with me, because I was in the corner, and Thomas was in the seat next to me, but one had put himself right beside Thomas.

We had nothing against gay guys or trannies. We were accustomed to them, since we traveled to and from the beach on Santa Monica Boulevard, where they were regulars, riding the bus or walking on the streets between La Brea and Fairfax Avenues. What made this interaction different was that they were messing with us. Patrick and Tim had hit their thighs back against the thighs of the gay guys and glared at them to let them know they weren't into what they were doing. But the men ignored the warning and kept testing and punking us. They were doing the same to Thomas. These guys were white, blond, and bigger and older than us; they weren't muscular, but looked fit enough that it would take two of us to take down one of them. So even though we were even in number, these guys had the advantage and they knew it.

Patrick, Tim, and Thomas had hatched a plan to get back at the gay guys who were rubbing themselves on them. The buses back then had emergency exits built into their large windows. There's a panel next to your shoulder that, if you pulled up, would release the bottom, freeing the window to swing from the top, which allowed you to exit. Patrick released the panel at one stop but didn't push the window open, then looked at Tim and Thomas while signaling me to get off the bus.

"Wait," I said. "This isn't our stop. We have several more blocks—"

"Shut up and get off the bus, man," Thomas said, looking at me intently and grabbing me by my arm. I didn't question any further; I knew they were up to something and it had to do with the gay guys.

"Bye, boys!" one of the gay guys said playfully, waving and smiling as we got off the bus through the back exit. As the rear exit doors of the bus closed, Tim opened the back window panel and held it up as Patrick, who carried a can of mace with him, yelled, "Fuck you, you fucking faggots!" while spraying all four of them.

The bus was moving forward, and as Patrick finished spraying them (luckily, it was mid-afternoon on a weekday and the bus was lightly occupied, with most passengers sitting near the front), the bus stopped. We could hear coughing intermixed with the cursing of "those little shit motherfuckers!" We laughed and ran in the opposite direction of the bus, knowing they were going to come after us when they recovered from the spraying.

We ran to the end of the next block. When we looked back we saw them get off. The bus happened to be in front of a liquor store where two transvestites were walking out, each carrying a case of beer. The four gay guys told them what happened, all while blinking rapidly and trying to wipe the mace from their faces, which was only making it worse. We could tell that the trannies were upset as they listened, because they glared at us. We gave them the middle finger, laughing, and yelling, "You fucking faggots!"

Our laughter turned into an "oh shit" moment when the trannies placed their cases of beer on the ground and started running toward us. Though they were wearing women's flat shoes, paired with skirts and tight tops, they were both black, tall, and very muscular. They definitely lifted weights.

"Damn, they run fast. Run, man!" exclaimed Tim, laughing at the danger.

We all started running in the opposite direction. Being younger and accustomed to running, even though we smoked cigarettes, we easily made it to the next block, and continued giving the two trannies the middle finger while laughing. Then, another gay couple walked past and looked at us, and the two black trannies yelled, "Those kids sprayed Rob and Steve!" (Their names weren't Rob and Steve; I don't recall their actual names.)

We looked at each other and started laughing harder. We were on Santa Monica Boulevard a few blocks west of Vine Street, in the middle of the gay/tranny hood. The gay couple walking past us turned and looked at us, but they were white and skinny, unlike the two muscular trannies who were now standing winded at the other end of the block. Patrick took out his mace and sprayed the couple as we ran to the next block. From there, we would have to either go north or south.

"This way!" shouted Tim. He turned south. We followed him through a smaller street away from Santa Monica Boulevard. "My friend lives a couple of blocks away. Follow me!"

We ran in a pack, looking over our shoulders every so often to see if we were still being followed. After a left on another small street, we made our way to the backyard of Tim's friend's house.

"Hey, what's up man? What brings you by?"

Tim's friend was Puerto Rican. I don't remember his name since that was our first and last meeting. He was tall, athletic, and had short curly brown hair with a light mustache. He wore a tank top with jeans. Tim told him what happened, and his friend started laughing. He volunteered to go out and look to see if anyone had followed or was looking for us.

He was gone for a while, so we sat around the backyard. The friend's younger sister came out and offered us water from plastic cups. After a while, Tim's friend came back with news.

"Yeah, they're looking for you guys. I spoke to my neighbor. He's gay but cool, and he says there's several carloads of guys out driving the neighborhood."

"What?" Tim was incredulous. None of us thought things would blow up into something like this. Our conversation moved from the back of the house to the side, and we saw a carload of guys drive by.

"That's one of them," Tim's friend said, pointing as they drove past. "My mom and dad are having a party in an hour; you guys can stick around until things cool off."

"Why not?" Patrick said. "Not like we have anywhere to be."

We met Tim's friend's parents, and Tim's friend told them what happened. The mom had a disapproving look on her face, but the father chuckled and said, "Shouldn't mess with kids, especially the ones that run around these neighborhoods, eh?"

"That's right," said Thomas as he pulled the red box of Marlboros from his shirt pocket and took out a cigarette.

Tim's friend's parents got their party started with music and food. As the guests arrived, we started intermingling with them. Eventually, the party spilled out front. Kids were playing on the street, and relatives and friends talked on the sidewalk or while going to the backyard for food and drinks. The family lived on a small enough street that hardly any cars went by. At least, not without a purpose…

A couple of times a carload of gay/tranny guys drove up, asking if anyone saw four kids, two Asian-looking and two Mexican-looking. Even though Tim was Egyptian, he easily passed for Hispanic. Everyone would say no, even though by this time, everyone at the party knew who we were and why we were there.

But when a car came around for the third time, Tim, being Tim, couldn't help himself. He interjected himself into the conversation with the carload of guys. "Yeah, I heard about what happened, and they might have gone in that direction."

He pointed west.

I knew what he was doing; he was trying to get them to go the opposite direction. We needed to go east to get back home.

"Wait a minute—weren't you one of the guys on the bus?"

One of the guys who was on the bus and got sprayed was sitting in the back seat. Five dudes were crammed in a compact car, and this guy was sitting directly behind the front passenger seat.

Tim was a quick thinker. He answered using an imitation of the slight Hispanic/Puerto Rican accent belonging to his friend's father. "Huh, what? I'm visiting my cousin who's having this party. I drove down here with my uncle. What you talking about?"

"Oh, sorry. You looked like one of the kids on the bus."

"What? Mang, that's messed up. I have a gay cousin. She look like a guy, pees standing up and I'm cool with it. I hope you get those guys. In fact, I want you to come back and get us when you find them. Okay?"

"Thanks, brother," said another passenger who was sitting behind the driver. It was one of the big black trannies that chased us. I don't know how he fit in that car, but I suppose those guys were on a mission and were willing to put up with a bit of discomfort.

Fortunately, it was evening, and with only the streetlights to see by, along with not getting a good look at us in the first place, we were pretty much in the clear. Patrick and I already knew we had to stay in the background and out of sight. We were the only two Asians at the party and stuck out.

"It's like that movie, *The Warriors*—trying to get home while being chased by rival gangs," Patrick said thoughtfully as we watched the car drive off.

"Yeah, but we're being chased by faggots," retorted Thomas as he lit up another cigarette and passed out a few for the rest of us.

"You look kind of young," a girl's voice said from behind me.

I turned around. It was Tim's friend's sister again, and she was looking at me. She was pretty, almost my height, and had curly brown hair, soft brown eyes, and wore a tank top and shorts that looked one size too small for her.

"Yeah," I said, trying not to stare too hard. "I'm the youngest."

"How old are you?"

"Fourteen."

"Me too. My mom and dad would never let me run around like you. I can't even take the bus by myself."

"That's because you're a girl and your older brother wouldn't let you either." Even though I just met her brother, I could tell that about him.

"I think your brother is looking for you," Tim said.

"Oh, okay." She turned and walked away.

That was abrupt. And how did Tim know anyway?

"Man," Tim said to me, "don't talk to her, and don't look at her."

"What? How come?"

"Her brother is overprotective. Plus, she's not into Asians."

"How do you know? She was talking to me."

"She's being nice. She's only using you to get to *me*."

Thomas rolled his eyes, and Patrick laughed.

"Yeah, all the ladies love me," Tim continued. "Plus, you got Shawnice." He laughed.

Shawnice was a girl from our neighborhood who lived in the same apartment complex as Tim. She was the same age as me, shy, black, pretty, and smelled like cocoa butter. I knew she liked me, but we could never complete a conversation because her older sister Connie was always hanging around close by, making it awkward and saying things like, "Oooh, Tony Mooooon, you like my sister? Shawnice, Tony Mooooon got them sexy legs, look at those hairs on them legs. Tony Mooooon, Shawnice says she's buying you Adidas cologne. I know she likes you…" And that would be the end of whatever conversation we tried having. I would mumble something about meeting Tim or Patrick, while feeling self-conscious about my legs and vowing never again to wear the Ocean Pacific brand shorts that came up halfway to my thigh.

We stayed at the party much longer than any of us expected. Those guys kept driving around the neighborhood into the latter part of the evening, hoping to catch one or all of us. Finally, as the party started winding down, one of the uncles of Tim's friend drove us back to our neighborhood in Hollywood.

Tim, Patrick, and I had a lot of fun together, and got in a lot of trouble. By the time I was initiated, though, we all parted ways. It was gradual, as we were making new friends from different gangs. But Patrick would later introduce me to Ricky, who would facilitate my joining BNG and would later become one of the four founders of my new crew: TGP.

CHAPTER FIVE

When I was sixteen, one of the main guys from BNG was shot and killed, and some of the older guys went to jail. So I helped start another crew with three other guys: Edgar, whose older brother was part of an allied Filipino gang called Jeffrox; Ricky, another BNG member; and Ronnie, a guy who hung out with a Hispanic gang called Rockwood Street in the heart of Koreatown. We called our new crew Tau Gamma Pinoy, which we took from an actual Filipino fraternity in the Philippines: Tau Gamma Phi, or TGP. We changed the Phi to Pinoy (which means Filipino) to differentiate ourselves from the fraternity.

We were a mix of guys—Hispanics, like Mexicans and Salvadorans, a couple of white guys, non-Filipino Asians like me, a few more Koreans, Thai, and Vietnamese. Guys joined for various reasons: friendship/camaraderie, girls, notoriety, or because they just wanted to hang out. My friend Ronnie used to joke that we took nerdy guys and turned them into thugs. Even though he was joking, I never felt good about that statement, since it was true to a certain degree. We quickly gained more members, often guys from other gangs that were slowly becoming inactive, usually because the older guys in those gangs were aging out and leaving the gang life, getting shot and killed, or in jail. We went from being a small group of guys that no one had heard of, to a gang that everyone was talking about, within six months. And six months after that, there were 150 of us, spread over four cities in Los Angeles County.

Looking back, it was so stupid, hating another group of guys because they were from another neighborhood, when they probably had the same characters we did: the clown who knew how to make you laugh with the craziest stories; the fighter; the smart guy who should be doing well in school yet was part of the group; the guy who always approached girls; the guy who always had girls approach him; and so on.

After three years of fighting, shooting, getting shot at, visiting friends in the hospital, and going to funerals with some of the guys talking about brokering firearms between the Salvadorans and the Chinatown gangs, I was ready to leave. Upon learning of this, some of the guys cried, and others wanted me beaten out of the gang—only they couldn't decide who would do it, since I had brought many of them in. But I knew it was time. I had a strange feeling of getting older, and I wanted to age out before turning eighteen, because at that point, if I were caught doing a crime, I would be tried as an adult with harsher criminal penalties and sentences.

But it wasn't just the legal penalties that bothered me. Even though our crew was "winning," it didn't *feel* like winning. I'd experienced the aftermath of losing one of our own or someone we knew. The anger, the sadness, the posturing, and the promised payback. All of this set against the backdrop of a devastated family. And the "homies" who said they were "down with you" only meant it while you were alive. A few months after you were gone, the only ones to visit your gravesite would be your family members.

I was no different. The hypocrisy within made it difficult to look at myself in the mirror.

Visiting one of the guys who got shot in the face by a rival gang with a shotgun full of birdshot added to my frustration with the senselessness of it all. He was fortunate it was birdshot and not buckshot. He took the blast while protecting his younger brother, pushing him ahead in front of him as they ran. When he turned to look back at the carload of guys, one of them raised his shotgun. The last thing he saw was the muzzle flash while running behind his brother. As they rounded a corner and lost the carload of guys, his face felt wet. When his brother saw him, the look on his face scared him more than getting shot.

At the hospital, I saw he had pockmarks on his face that looked similar to chickenpox. One of the bits of birdshot had landed close to his left eye, and the doctor didn't take it out because it would've been too close to his optic nerve, so it was left in. The rest were removed.

The brothers got their payback sometime later, and the older brother ended up joining the Marines to get away from the cycle. But that was how it went. It was a never-ending pattern, a perpetual war. Someone got offended, someone shot at someone, someone got shot at, and often for reasons that many couldn't remember after some time.

If it wasn't external forces trying to do us in, we had to contend with the fight we had within ourselves. Many of us were broken inside. We came from broken homes of single parents, had strained relationships like the one I had with my father, or were raised by grandparents because our parents, for various reasons, found it inconvenient to take care of their own children. The crew provided what many of us didn't get at home: attention and connection.

The emotional pain would at times manifest itself in ways that involved harming oneself. It wasn't uncommon for members to cut themselves, and we'd accept it as just the way things were, not recognizing that these were signs of deep emotional hurt and deficiencies. I'd find myself doing the same, deriving a sense of satisfaction from making the cuts on my arm and watching the blood gather and pool into drops, fascinated by the pain and the vivid red color.

Sometimes these emotions led to a tragic end. We heard of a rival that hanged himself after breaking up with his girl; he was high on some kind of drug plus alcohol. No one laughed or joked. Even though it wasn't one of us, it could've been, and later, it was.

Russel was only sixteen, and lived with his grandfather and older brother because his mother and father didn't want him. He was two years younger than me at the time and very chatty. I mean *constantly* talking. There was never a time when I was around him when I didn't hear his voice. Russel was my personal herald, announcing my arrival and departure.

"Here he comes, our beloved T, the OG, our *veterano*, make way *pared*, move!" he'd announce loud enough for everyone near us to hear. "Pared" is Tagalog for "dude" or "bro." A typical greeting is "*Oy, Kumusta ka pared*?" (translated to hey, what's up man?)

Later, I would miss that voice. His girlfriend broke up with him after a year of going out. They were always together, and many thought they'd get married after high school or that his girlfriend would get pregnant before graduating. Two months after the breakup, he shot himself with a shotgun. I didn't go to the funeral because I was already out of TGP and wanted to avoid questions from my former crew, but I knew his grandfather and brother. His grandfather owned a small hole-in-the-wall retail shop selling things like candy, ice cream, and cigarettes. A week after the funeral, I went by the store, and his older brother was present along with his grandfather. His older brother was twenty years old and attending UCLA.

With my head hung low, I stood in front of the store and cried, mumbling that I was sorry. Russel's grandfather started crying too and asked me to leave in a hoarse whisper. His older brother, through tears in his eyes, was gracious enough to tell me that it wasn't me but the situation. "We're all hurting. Come back another time."

I never did. But my friend Perry went with Russel's grandfather and brother to visit the gravesite. On occasion, Russel's ex-girlfriend would also be there. No one blamed her; she was broken too. We all were.

Leaving TGP didn't mean I was no longer considered an enemy to rival crews. My girlfriend's brother, an older main guy from a rival gang called Satanas, or STS, helped broker a peace with me and several rival gangs. It was tenuous, but the news spread that as long as I didn't "claim" my previous affiliation with TGP, they would uphold the agreement.

I couldn't venture freely throughout L.A.—some would view it as an insult if I showed up in their neighborhood—and I had to stay vigilant when I was out. The war between my former crew and others was ongoing. There were pictures of me and some of my crew being circulated, and it was always an uneasy feeling when someone I'd just met already knew me. Reputation created an unrealistic image of me being untouchable, and there was always someone who wanted to test that.

CHAPTER SIX

By the time I turned seventeen, I had already been to juvenile hall and worked off more than two hundred hours of community service. I had been arrested for some petty graffiti (even though they wanted to get me for so much more, with suspicion that my crew was responsible for the recent increase in violence on the streets). I would have preferred just doing my time in juvenile hall and being done with it, but my father asked the judge for community service, stating that juvenile hall would be a learning and training center, not a place to rehabilitate someone like me.

He was right. During the two weeks I was held until my court date, I had already made friends with the Hispanics. One of them had a large "F13" tattoo on his chest, which I recognized as Florencia 13, a generational Mexican gang that called Huntington Park and South Gate their home. I hung out with the younger brother of one of their guys, since my father owned a market in Huntington Park after selling the one he had in Boyle Heights. Soon I was eating with them, lifting weights with them, and generally hanging with them until my court date. Those gang ties would have only strengthened had I stayed any longer.

Community service sucked, and there were many times I wished I was incarcerated instead. But my father knew that long-term incarceration would have opened a whole new world for me, with connections and opportunities. The wrong kind. So he took me to the probation office in Santa Monica (a forty-five-minute drive from Hollywood, even with light traffic) at eight a.m. every Saturday and Sunday to paint over graffiti or hoe areas overgrown with brush. When I got home, I'd shower, leaving behind a thin layer of dirt. On the days we were clearing brush, which was most of the time, I'd blow out dirt boogers, too. It was physically intensive work under the sun, with only short breaks for water and a longer one for lunch—brown-bagged bologna or ham sandwiches provided by the county.

The probation officer was an African gentleman who drove an older Toyota Cressida and always talked about how it was the best buy he'd ever made. Sometimes he'd reference a quote he claimed was from Hitler—"a man doesn't need to show his teeth." It meant don't smile too much. But in reality, that was contradictory to his demeanor. He was almost *always* smiling. Plus, I'm not sure if Hitler ever said that. Overall, though, I think the officer actually enjoyed the company of the young men who were working off their sentences with community service.

One of those young men was a black kid from the Hoover Crips. We were within his gang's territory one Saturday, getting rid of graffiti on the wall. "Getting rid of it" meant painting over it, unless the wall was porous like cinderblock, in which case it was sandblasted. We were also cautioned not to get too close to any parked cars while we worked, because the fine grains of sand would ricochet with enough force to chip the vehicles' paint. If the graffiti was near any cars, we had to ask the car owner to move it, or we'd just skip it.

We came across graffiti that this kid's gang had left behind—and so we automatically knew who was going to paint over it. The African probation officer delighted in watching anyone paint over their crew's graffiti and the rest of us laughed as he reluctantly painted over it.

The kid had the saddest look, but the probation officer had a huge smile on his face. In his African accent, he'd offer "encouragement."

"Yeah, don't forget that spot right there, yeah, right there." He'd point and smile.

Even though we were sometimes painting over our crew, we couldn't help but smile in return. I'm sure no one told their crew this story when they returned home.

For the most part, gang affiliations were ignored within the group doing community service, since we knew the alternative was getting sent to juvenile hall, which no one except me seemed to want to do. But then, my feelings on that would change, depending on the day. It was a hate/tolerate sort of relationship. Some days were light, like when we were painting, and on those days, I relished my freedom. But on those weekends where we would clear the brush, I would seriously reconsider community service in favor of doing time.

There were rare occasions when a fight would start between two rivals, but that never occurred while I was present. For the most part, everyone kept that to themselves. After our time was done, the county van returned to the parking lot of the probation office, and a few of us would stick around, smoking cigarettes and talking about what we'd done to end up getting assigned to community service until we were told to go home.

My bus ride back from Santa Monica to Hollywood was about an hour and a half. When I got home, I was physically and mentally exhausted. After my shower, I'd fall asleep thinking it would be a short nap, but would wake up at three a.m. and miss hanging out with everyone. I suppose the county designed it that way so kids like me would be too tired to do anything in the evenings on the weekend.

That was a good thing because my probation also included house arrest, which meant that during the week, I was only allowed to leave the house to go to school. This was before ankle monitors, and you had to be near a landline phone when your probation officer called. I developed a workaround for that.

After school, I would go home, then meet some of the guys to play basketball at the school across the street from our apartment. Since the gates were locked, we had to scale two nine-foot-high fences—and one was closer to eleven feet, since it was placed on top of a two-foot concrete wall. When the probation officer called, my father would walk up the driveway of the apartment and yell for me. I'd hop the two fences and run past him as he scolded, "Hurry up!" in Korean as I entered the apartment to pick up the phone.

"What took so long, and why are you breathing heavy?" the probation officer once asked.

"I was in the shower and trying to finish up to get to the phone."

"You're in the shower every time I call."

"When I get back from school, I want to get cleaned up, so I take my time cleaning every nook and cranny, to make me clean as a whistle." I imitated a whistle from a popular soap commercial at the time, for Irish Spring.

"Smartass. Get to the phone sooner and don't keep me waiting next time."

I think my probation officer probably had an idea that I wasn't at home but was at least nearby. Still, as long as I made it to the phone quick enough, he couldn't say much. I'm glad he didn't do physical visits. I just had to stay out of trouble at school and in public to stay under his radar.

The trouble with that was… I had a history of getting into trouble, even back when my mother was still alive.

CHAPTER SEVEN

My father knew I would thrive in a prison environment, and not in the way he wanted. I had a way of working through challenges.

He would often bring up an incident from when I was a boy. It was his favorite.

At seven years old, I'd come home from school and call my parents at the market to let them know that I was home. They had a term for kids like me during the late 1970s and 1980s: "latchkey kids." With no parents around until later in the evening, we were left unsupervised for hours. After finishing my homework (which took less than an hour), the rest of my time was spent watching TV until my parents came home. Even with the limited channels back then, there was always something to watch. My favorite show was *Get Smart*, a spoof on the spy genre at the time, with Maxwell Smart, a bumbling spy who somehow still won the day, had a shoe telephone, and was accompanied by an attractive female spy, Agent 99.

My father wasn't happy that I was watching so much TV, especially when I lied about not watching. As a drastic measure, he cut the cord at the connector with a kitchen knife. But within a couple of days, I stripped the rubber insulation from the wires with the same kitchen knife, exposed the wires, then inserted the wires into the wall. I'd learned this by watching my father do some handyman work on wiring. Aside from the spark the wires created when inserted into the socket, everything went fine: the TV worked. And each day when it was about time for my parents to come home, I'd tuck the cord under the TV to hide the stripped ends and make it appear as if it were still haphazardly tossed aside by my father.

My deception worked until one unusually cool week. Our 1970s big-box Zenith TV emitted heat, which wasn't noticeable when the weather was warm. But when the weather was cooler, and I had the TV on from three thirty in the afternoon to almost ten at night… well, it made a difference. I was careful to turn the TV off thirty minutes before they came home, but the warmth inside the apartment was noticeable, especially without a heater.

My parents were flabbergasted when they realized what I'd done. My mother was stupefied that I'd stripped the cord. She repeated, "He could've burnt the place down!" over and over in Korean.

After recovering from his shock, my father was pissed beyond belief. The punishment for a situation like this one went beyond the usual spanking. When my father reached the very end of his patience, he would fill the bathtub with cold water and tell me to strip down to my underwear—then he would swear that he would drown me. While he was filling the tub, I would find a way to escape from the bathroom. The best one was when I told him that I wanted to say a few words to my mother before my demise, to which he made me promise that I'd come back afterward. I swore up and down that I would. I didn't.

It would turn into a chase to try and catch me, since I would run around the apartment like a half-naked monkey, ducking under the table, grabbing on to my mother's legs, and jumping from one bed to another. I don't know where my father got the idea for that punishment, but it never worked, since eventually, he'd get tired of cursing and chasing me. Then he would accept my crying apology with the promise that "I'll never do it again."

That was, until I did something else later that got me into trouble again.

If I wasn't creating problems at home, then I was doing so at school. If the problems were big enough, my parents were called to a meeting with the teacher—and every so often, with the principal. My parents were probably called in to the school every other month, on average.

I wasn't always the one starting trouble. There was, for example, the time a black kid named Keith urinated on my pants. We were both using the urinal trough—a common sight in the boys' bathroom in the 1970s. We had to stand next to each other in a row as we peed into it. Keith amused himself by spraying his piss left and right in the trough, and on this occasion, it escaped containment and hit the side of my pants. He thought that was funny, and started laughing. I didn't. I zipped up and, without thinking twice or hesitating, punched him in the face in the middle of a laugh that immediately went from low whine to loud crying.

The teacher sent me to the principal's office. But the principal didn't seem too upset; he was almost understanding. Even though my parents had to come to the office the next day, my father was okay with what I'd done this time, too. There was no spanking or attempted drowning session awaiting me that evening, thankfully. Nobody likes being involuntarily pissed on.

Keith and I actually became friends after that, finding a connection playing marbles, until he moved away when the school year was over. I can laugh about it now. My father's threats of drowning… not so much. But neither do I hold it against him.

I never thought about going to therapy to cry about how my father tried to drown me. I was a pain in the neck, and he was at his wits' end with a kid who was continually getting into one form of trouble or another. And when my mother passed away, I got into much more serious trouble, and he never gave up on me. I was his son, and he never wavered from his responsibility as a father.

That's a lesson that still resonates with me today, as a father myself. I hesitated to have kids for a long time, because there was no way I wanted to raise a kid who was like me. Thank you, God, that didn't happen.

CHAPTER EIGHT

After the TV cord incident, I wasn't left alone at home anymore, and my mother would take me with her to work at the family market. My parents initially didn't want me there because of the neighborhood. Boyle Heights is considered the armpit of East Los Angeles. Its demographic is mainly low-income, newly arrived immigrants (both legal and illegal), with multiple street gangs, the biggest being Big Hazard gang, or BH for short. I had to stay inside the store doing homework and reading books checked out from the school library, but I was yearning to go outside. No warning, threats, or physical punishment could keep me from joining the rest of the neighborhood kids… and fighting with them.

It was the late 1970s, and I was a skinny Korean kid with a bowl haircut that made me look like a small Bruce Lee. I was getting into fights on a weekly basis, sometimes two or three times a week, over being called a *chinito* (that's "little Chinaman" in Spanish). When it wasn't that, it was usually some dispute over a game, usually *canicas* ("marbles" in Spanish). I quickly learned that the problem with fighting one Mexican kid was the rest of his siblings and extended family. Even when I "won" the fight, I was going to lose because I'd have to fight an older and bigger sibling or cousin afterward.

Most of my fights were against my friend Beto. I think his full name was Alberto, but everyone called him Beto for short, and I did, too. He was a fat Mexican kid who probably outweighed me by thirty to forty pounds and was slightly taller than me. Beto was not only big for his age, he was also really ugly. Short, disheveled hair, cut out of necessity not style; two front teeth curved inward and slightly crooked, giving him a rodent-like appearance; a bunch of freckles on a face that was broad but compressed from the top, making him look like he could pass for Asian—Filipino at the least.

Beto enjoyed annoying me, and I enjoyed annoying him; we were little assholes to each other. One fight started over, of all things, potato chips! I didn't know that Lay's Sour Cream and Onion chips were *supposed* to have those tiny green flakes on them; I thought the chips accidentally fell on the grass. When Beto heard this, he got up, walked across the front porch where we were hanging out, and laughed in my face, saying I was a chinito and the slant in my eyes made me partially blind.

Thinking about it now, that's pretty funny, but back then, I wasn't having it. I went from zero to rage in less than a second and punched him in the face close to his jaw. Then we were both tumbling over the front porch railing to land on the grass on Beto's front lawn, still punching each other. Beto's brother —also named Tony—had to break it up. He was across the street while I was mounted on Beto, grabbing the side of his head by his hair and pounding it onto the grass. Tony came running over, exasperated with us both for going at it so often.

We couldn't help it. Everything we did resulted in a fight, but we both must have enjoyed it, because we still would hang out.

Our friendship deepened on a summer day when the kids from our neighborhood went to the local Boys and Girls Club in Boyle Heights to go swimming. That made things easier on my mom, who could drop me off and work at the market. Even though I didn't live in the neighborhood, I was there so often that it felt like I did; we only would go back to Hollywood when the store closed at 10pm. All the Mexicans and Chicanos (Mexicans born in the US, mainly California) from different neighborhoods were there, with me being the only Korean kid. Two kids at the club saw me and one made a remark. "Look! A chinito!"

My first thought was that once I got into this fight, swimming at the club wasn't going to be an option anymore, and I really wanted to keep swimming. But I also wanted to fight this kid for disrespecting me like that.

But it was Beto who responded first from behind me. "What? So what's up, then? You got a problem?"

The rest of the kids from our neighborhood overheard, since we were all moving together around the game room area as a group, and started to close in on the two kids. The two kids had friends too, and we saw them turn to face us as well. Two groups of kids from different neighborhoods were gathered to see how this was going to play out.

The other guys backed down. "Okay, it's cool."

Everyone relaxed and the two groups went from being on the brink of a fight to playing like old friends. Whenever we got together to play pool, foosball, table tennis, or just hang out, from that day forward, I was still a chinito, but I was a chinito that belonged to a group. I was *their* chinito, and I became a little pain in the neck like the rest of the neighborhood kids my parents tried to prevent me from playing with.

Before cell phones and game consoles, we spent our time inventing mischievous ways to entertain ourselves. We'd join the older kids, who always came up with crazy ideas, like stealing eggs from the local market, which morphed into telling me to bring two dozen eggs from my parents' market. I did the job by telling my parents some of the kids' parents were going to bake a cake. I was such a little liar when I was young. It amazed my parents that I could make up a lie on the fly without much effort.

With eggs in hand, we positioned ourselves in the alley behind the Shell gas station and pelted random people as they put gas in their car. It was mainly the older kids throwing the eggs; the younger kids would laugh. The best was when a driver would get upset and run toward the incline to the alley for a little payback, and we'd all run in different directions, still laughing.

Beto and I still fought on occasion, but it wasn't anything like the first year I knew him. I think that's largely because another friend's uncle—a guy in his twenties who was part of a local gang called Fickett Street—told him to be cool with me. This was out of respect for my father. Many of the families relied on food stamps, and often it wasn't enough to cover expenses into the month, so my father extended credit to families he knew by simply keeping track of what they purchased, using one long blank side from a deconstructed cigarette carton. Doing business in a low-income neighborhood carries its own set of rules on how to interact with the customers to make a situation work for everyone.

The uncle in question once had an out-of-town cousin who broke into the market after we had closed. The neighborhood respect for my father was so great, that this Fickett Street gang member paid for the stolen beers and the broken window. That respect for my father carried over to me.

Many years later, around 2005, when I was early into my mortgage career, a Mexican co-worker named Robert turned to me, suddenly serious, and said, "Moon, I know my people, and on behalf of my people, I just want to say 'I'm sorry.'" He placed his right hand on his chest as a solemn gesture of apology on behalf of all Mexican and Chicano people who had mistreated me growing up.

I should've made a spectacle since we were at work and loudly proclaimed that I accepted his apology on behalf of all the Asians in America wronged by Mexicans. Instead I laughed, unsure if he was really serious or just messing with me.

"Moon! C'mon, man, I'm serious."

That made me laugh even harder. Then he started laughing too. Having lived in L.A. now for close to fifty years, I can say that Mexicans are some of my favorite people.

But it was my Korean friends who would be with me during the riots of 1992.

CHAPTER NINE

I made my first long-term Korean friends in the summer of 1989. I'd had a couple of Korean guys in my former crew, but they didn't hang out consistently. Since I missed so many classes during the regular school year at Hollywood High, they offered makeup classes at Fairfax High for the summer. It was there that I met Mitch and Marty.

I hit them up with the question of their gang affiliation —"Where you from?"—to which they responded RBS (Rebel Boys), an ally of my first gang. RBS was toning down their activity, since many of them were getting older.

Mitch lived near the Hollywood Hills, a few blocks north of Franklin Avenue, not far from me. He should've gone to Hollywood High, but since he lived in Koreatown before moving to Hollywood, they let him stay in the same school district. Mitch's oldest brother was from the Korean Killers (KK for short), a Koreatown gang known for their hand-to-hand fighting skills and being at odds with the Filipino and Chinatown gangs. They started in the early and mid-1970s, like many of the other Asian gangs of young immigrant men newly arrived and trying to adjust to the rules of living in Los Angeles.

Knowledge of KK's fighting skills and reputation carried outside of Koreatown. One of their main rivals was the Filipino gang STS, or Satanas. STS, also formed in the 1970s, was an offshoot of an older Hispanic gang in the Rampart area of Los Angeles, called Temple Street, since a majority of them lived around or near Temple Street. STS was the oldest Filipino gang in Los Angeles, and some of its members started other Filipino gangs throughout different parts of L.A.

Mitch's brothers were considered the "cool" Korean kids. Both had fast cars—the oldest brother drove a Chevy Camaro IROC, and the middle brother a Mazda RX-7—and girls were attracted to them. They had the appearance of the typical rich, good-looking high school guys.

Marty's family was different. They lived in Koreatown and owned a stall in a swap meet. Marty's older brother was a social misfit without friends and hung out at arcades playing video games. He was skinny, not good-looking, and socially awkward. He would sometimes hang out with us and remind us that he was the oldest, so we had to listen to him. (Korean male hierarchy depends on age; the older person holds the seniority.) Even though he sometimes tried to pull rank as the oldest, Marty's older brother wasn't intimidating. The fact that all of the younger kids could kick his ass is most likely what made him cool with us treating him as an equal—remember, age matters greatly in Korean culture—and referring to him by his first name made him our equal. Even so, I gave him space, acknowledging that he was Marty's older brother to avoid confrontation or challenging him, because I didn't want to put Marty in an awkward position.

But Mitch *did* butt heads with Marty's older brother at times, reminding him that *his* older brother (the middle brother in Mitch's family; Mitch was the youngest) used to push Marty's older brother around when they both attended Fairfax High. Mitch was like that sometimes, playing a game of "who's better." For a short period of time, he even called himself the "Dominator"—until I asked him what he dominated, laughing at him. He didn't speak to me for a day, but got over it.

Marty, Mitch, and I didn't make it to the end of our summer-school classes. Old habits die hard, and we often ended up skipping class to hang out on Melrose Avenue. Or sometimes Mitch would go "fishnapping" with his friend Arnie.

Arnie was almost two years younger, a unique character, and also a member of RBS. He was a skinny kid, but you'd never guess it. Why? He'd layer on his clothes, wearing four shirts and three pairs of pants to "bulk" himself up. This was a daily routine, even during the height of summer. We would be at school outside at the tennis courts in the ninety-degree summer heat, and he was sweating as if sitting in a sauna.

We all knew why and would poke at him about it when we got bored.

"Yo, Arnie, let's go to the beach next week," I'd say.

"No, I don't like the beach," he'd reply.

"What? You're Filipino. You guys are surrounded by water, and I know you like seafood."

"Yeah, I like seafood, but not the beach."

"Why?"

I'd pretend to be clueless to watch him squirm, and see his brain working overtime like a hamster on caffeine running on a wheel to come up with an answer in front of all of us. We all knew his only reason for layering was so he didn't look like the skinniest guy in our group—and to impress the halfway good-looking girls. If a girl was about a 6 out of 10, he'd make that play and approach them; shame was not in his character.

When Arnie was learning to drive, Mitch would sit in the passenger seat. Arnie would get distracted by a girl walking or sitting at the bus stop, turn his head, and ignore whatever was in front of the car. Mitch got really good at grabbing the steering wheel from the passenger seat, maneuvering while scolding him.

"Hey, Arnie, keep your eyes on the road, man!"

"Oh, right. Mitch, did you see her? She was fine!"

"So what? Just fucking drive, man!"

"Let's go back. I want to talk to her."

Then he'd make a U-turn at the next intersection. Girls liked him because he had a babyish face and would talk them up on how "fine" they were.

He now has five kids from three mothers, and two of the mothers are cousins. He's that guy who belongs on a talk show like Jerry Springer, with three baby mommas and girlfriends that suddenly show up in the middle of the show. As crazy as that sounds, he's a great father, and his kids love him. He never shirked his responsibilities as a father, always working long hours and dealing with issues from the mothers.

We got into a routine that summer, with Mitch picking me up in the morning, and then heading over to Arnie to pick him up. Picking up Arnie was a pain in the neck. We'd show up at 7:30 a.m. and have to wait twenty or thirty minutes, during which time Mitch and I would take turns yelling up to his third-story apartment window, telling him to hurry up. Arnie would occasionally pop his head out the window, yelling that he was almost ready. We'd threaten that we were leaving but we never did. This continued to be our morning routine even after summer school, when the regular semester started.

Sometimes Arnie's grandfather or grandmother would yell down at us that he was almost done. He'd lived with his grandparents since he was about two years old. I always felt bad for him because of that—it must suck to have both parents agree it would be better if the grandparents raised you. That was probably why I never really got upset with him, and when his grandfather or grandmother yelled that he'd be down soon, that would buy him another ten minutes. His grandparents were very nice, always asking if I'd eaten. They'd feed me anytime I'd visit. It's a Filipino thing, and the common phrase I'd hear walking into their home would be "Kumain ka ba" (*Did you eat?*).

Back then, we got into plenty of trouble, but the kind of trouble we got into wasn't universal. Take the aforementioned "fishnapping," for example. That was a Mitch and Arnie thing. The word itself was meant to soften what it really was—stealing fish from a pet store. The guys also thought it was funny to say. The two of them were really into a fish breed called cichlids. They were aggressive, highly territorial, and came in a variety of colors, but they were expensive for kids who didn't have a job or rich parents.

With Mitch's family, at least, you might get the impression that they had a lot of money. Mitch's brothers drove nice cars and *looked* rich, but everyone in his family worked, including his brothers, and contributed to the housing expenses. It was a shared effort. Mitch's mom would give him five dollars for lunch, and Arnie's grandparents did too. My father did the same, but that money was gone by noon or early afternoon, spent on cigarettes and snacks.

And so if, for some reason, you still wanted to buy these expensive fish and weren't willing to work a job, you went fishnapping.

Here's how fishnapping worked: Mitch and Arnie would keep a bucket of treated water for fish in the car, then drive to a pet fish store. Many were mom-and-pop shops owned by Asians who were clueless as to what Mitch and Arnie were doing. Now when it comes to the prized fish in question—cichlids—if you press and run your fingers across their tank, they'll follow your fingers. So, you just run your fingers to the top to bring them close to the edge of the aquarium… and then you grab one and put it in your pocket. It was ridiculously easy. They would do this several times, each time heading out to the car, dropping the fish in the bucket, and going back into the store for another.

Having a pet fish didn't interest me. The water smelled, and watching them swim didn't have that soothing effect on me that everyone talked about. But getting into trouble did appeal to me, so I went with them and tried fishnapping once, but just got the front of my pants wet. Besides, stealing didn't really appeal to me.

When I was six, I took a couple of toys from a supermarket —a small ball and a pair of plastic handcuffs. I forgot about them and left them in the pocket of my pants. My parents found them in my pocket the next morning. I got my first spanking in America for that, and I'll never forget it. It was difficult to sit properly for the next couple of days. The worst part was going back to the supermarket and returning the items, apologizing to the manager under the stern gaze of both my parents. It was an act of love and correction, but it felt so unloving at that time.

Mitch and Arnie almost got caught when Arnie's pants were drenched and the old Asian lady owner was watching him with a puzzled look on her face. I told them both we had to leave, then I strolled through the fish store looking at the other fish, waiting for them. That was the last time I went with them, but I know they kept it up, because when I went to their places after, the number of fish in their tank had grown to fifteen, and that was when I stopped counting. Their fish tank looked like the ones in the fish stores, teeming with a variety of cichlids.

I figure the store owners never suspected their fish were getting stolen because Mitch and Arnie were probably the first to do such a thing. Besides, many Asian owners never suspected Asian kids of stealing from them.

Stealing carried into their early twenties, when the two of them worked together at an office supply retail chain that's no longer around. They'd toss printers, scanners, and other electronics—still in their boxes—into the large outside trash bin. Then, after the store closed, they'd come back to pick up their loot. Mitch's oldest brother found out what they were doing and told them both to stop. That was the end of that.

CHAPTER TEN

The summer of 1989 set the pattern for how we'd hang out for the next year and a half. After school, or if we all skipped our classes, we'd end up at Marty's house in the evenings—but not before hanging out at the Boys and Girls Club in Hollywood.

The Boys and Girls Club of Hollywood was a long-established venue just south of Sunset Boulevard and Wilton Avenue, on a small street called De Longpre Avenue. I was introduced to the place in 1980, at eight years old. At the end of that school year, my parents decided I would spend the summer at the Boys Club. Back then, the boys and girls had different clubs, separated by a large swimming pool that was shared by both.

The club had a two-month summer program where you were given lunch and could participate in different activities, mostly games like pool, foosball, or table tennis, or playing outside on a softball field lined with eucalyptus trees that gave a distinct smell to the field during the spring and summer. They also had a second-floor art/drawing area overseen by a counselor who taught drawing lessons, mainly of Marvel characters. One time, the counselor made a life-size drawing of what the Incredible Hulk would look like if he were real. It was placed at the stairwell landing between the first set of stairs and the second, so we were greeted by the Hulk as we made our way up.

There aren't many places like that for kids anymore. The Boys and Girls Club of Hollywood was sold to Home Depot, and that's what's there as of this writing.

When my mother first took me to look into that 1980 summer program, she went to the office to find out how much it would cost. It turned out to be more than my parents could afford, and I would have to wait for the next summer. But as we were leaving, an older white lady who was also in the office visiting her friend (the lady who was giving my mother the information) overheard their conversation—and paid for my summer program. I wish I could remember her name; she even gave me a birthday card that year.

She was a real estate agent from Coldwell Banker; I remember that bit of information from her business card. My eight-year-old mind wanted to know what this lady did for a living that could make her so generous to an eight-year-old Korean kid with a bowl haircut.

She gave me a summer experience I'd never forget. I would thank her profusely if we met in person again.

I joined the softball league at the Boys Club and ended up on Nate's team. Nate was in his mid to late twenties, a trim, athletic black guy, about five-foot-eight with Jheri curls and a cool disposition. His face naturally rested into a smile, and it eased all the boys. Nate was loved by all of us, and this was why, every year, Nate's team would win. Which is actually why I was on the team to begin with. That year, Nate had the last pick in the rotation, and that was where I was chosen.

I learned so much from Nate that year, especially about teamwork, camaraderie, and how to be encouraging. Even when you struck out, he'd say, "That's okay, baby, we're okay." (Modern readers should know that "baby" was late '70s / early '80s slang, so please don't read in any "pedo" connotations.) Nate would say all this while clapping and telling the next guy to get up to bat.

He had a way with kids. Even during practice, we worked hard just to have him say, "That's right on, baby, keep it going."

I'd never met anyone quite like Nate, even to this day. He was always easy-going and calm. He never yelled at us or called us losers, which was a surprisingly common thing to do to kids playing sports back in the 80s. Nothing seemed to disturb him. But I do recall one loss when we really disappointed him: the older kids didn't take the game seriously and were goofing off, which led the younger kids, like me, to follow their lead. In the middle of the game, Nate spoke to us. I don't recall all of his words, because I was eight and had the attention span of a gnat, but it was serious, and the consternation in his voice was enough to slap the goofiness out of all of us. From that point on, everyone was so focused that it didn't feel like a game, but a military operation. Guys on the bench were standing and staring intently, giving us looks of "You better get this right." There was way more pressure from my teammates when I got up to bat than there was from Nate, with his easygoing smile, clapping and saying, "Let's go, baby, you got this." If I messed up, Nate would be cool, but everyone else wasn't going to give me a "pass" or be cool like Nate.

Somehow I ended up as the catcher. Everyone had to play, and that was probably the only position that was safe enough for me not to mess things up. I knew how to catch a ball with a glove and throw it back, because my father would practice with me on occasion. But most of the kids on the team were older, maybe ten or eleven years old. Our pitcher was eleven, and he would cover for me when we had a runner on third base or I got knocked over when someone would run or slide into home plate.

We finished in first place that season. I'd never won a trophy before that day, but each member of my team came away with one. Afterward, we took a bus ride to a pizza party at Shakey's Pizza on Sunset Boulevard and Normandie Avenue.

Years later, I saw Nate on the bus. He didn't recognize me until I told him who I was. Like a street thug, I was wearing large, baggy clothes, plus I had a mustache and a pompadour hairstyle with long hair in the back, a far cry from the bowl-cut eight-year-old kid he'd coached years before. After reminiscing about the past for a bit, and asking me about my personal circumstances, he told me I was going in the wrong direction with my life. Then his stop came up. He took a long look at me, and before he parted, he placed his left hand on my shoulder and said, "You take care of yourself, okay?"

That struck me deeply. The look he gave me stayed with me, even to this day.

It was all part of the events that led me to exit that lifestyle. It didn't fit me anymore. The person who'd impacted my life so positively at eight years old did it again nine years later. Meeting him on that bus was not a coincidence; it was part of God's plan to change the trajectory of my life.

I went back to the Boys Club again in 1981, when I was nine. My parents had enough money this time, for both the summer program and the week-long summer camp in July that was held with several other Boys Clubs in Los Angeles. The camp had a lake for fishing, and we would use pieces of American cheese, the square ones that come in their own wrappers, as bait. Then we'd release the fish back into the lake. There was also a swimming pool, and in the evening, each cabin would perform skits by a large campfire. There were probably seventy or eighty kids running around that camp, with each cabin assigned a group name and its own counselor.

My mother thought I was a bit young, but she was reassured that there were younger kids than me going. My cabin had an eight-year-old skinny white kid that everyone liked, and I felt relieved not to be the youngest kid in the group. Side note: That kid took a crap in the showers near the end of the week of our trip. The showers had an open layout, just everyone naked in a large room with individual shower heads. He took a crap right in the center because he couldn't make it to the toilet. Maybe the hot water relaxed him? Who knows. And who knows why he did it right in the center. I asked him what happened, and he just said he couldn't hold it. But I wonder if one of the older kids dared him, telling him it would be funny. Those kinds of dares were fairly common.

Our counselor, who was from the Hollywood Boys Club, was livid. What made it more memorable was he was the only counselor with a Tom Selleck mustache. So imagine Magnum P.I. yelling at all of us, “Who was the fucking idiot that took a shit in the shower!”

That was how he put it. The 80’s were a different time.

We liked the skinny white kid, so nobody said anything, and we all feigned ignorance. The timing of the counselor’s rant couldn’t have been better since it occurred during the middle of movie night. They paused the movie over the commotion, turned on the lights, and then all the counselors were furious, with ours yelling at the guys from our cabin about how they had to clean it up. Meanwhile, the skinny white kid wore a “please don’t tell on me” expression on his face.

For some reason, they didn’t force our entire cabin to do the cleanup, but we did have to stand by and miss movie night as our counselor went to work. We had a hard time trying not to laugh when the counselor ranted about the stink and how it kept smearing. I don’t know why he shared the details, but it still makes me chuckle thinking about it to this day. We were sent back to our cabin while everyone else finished the movie.

The next day, the guilty kid bought bags of Doritos from the camp store for everyone in our cabin. What a cool kid—

regardless of the fact that he took a crap in the middle of the shower room.

I didn't go back to the Boys Club until years later, hanging with my crew. It was a different place by then. The demographic of the kids had changed, and now they were mainly Hispanic. That was consistent with the surrounding neighborhood, which had gone from a diverse mix of white, black, Asian, and Hispanic of various socioeconomic backgrounds to becoming predominantly lower-income Hispanic. I think that may have affected the funding, which would help explain why they combined the boys and girls into one club. Nate was long gone, but the art/drawing counselor was still there.

Unfortunately for the club, it became a focal point for fights with rival gangs out in the street and the neighboring shopping plaza. It got so bad that one of the counselors who knew me, the one with the Tom Selleck mustache, told me our presence posed a threat and danger to the younger boys. He was asking me to do the right thing. I understood; every week, there was something, and LAPD were present daily, either patrolling or parked down the block. I told my crew, and we left.

When I showed my face again the following year with Mitch, Marty, and Arnie to hang out after our summer school classes, the Tom Selleck-mustached counselor wasn't exactly thrilled to see me. He asked point blank if these were the same guys from my old crew, thinking we were there to cause trouble again.

I told him I had left that life behind and was trying to go "straight." I was welcomed back with my new friends. But going straight wasn't in my immediate future, no matter what I told the counselor. It was this not-so-straight path that would lead me onto the chaotic and lawless streets of L.A., three years later.

CHAPTER ELEVEN

We met Carlo at around that time. Actually, it was Marty who met him first, through an after-school program they both attended at a church in Koreatown. Carlo's parents were well off; they owned a two-story craftsman house and had a maid who made sandwiches for us when we hung out there. He was the middle child, with one brother two years older, and one almost ten years younger. His older brother was trying to join the LAPD, and Carlo was going to a community college, Valley College in the San Fernando Valley, to finish his general education classes before picking a major and transferring. His parents owned a well-known Salvadoran restaurant in the Pico Union district of L.A. that was popular with the local Salvadoran community. Carlo was the only non-Asian in our group.

When I first met Carlo, I thought he might be gay. He had curly-ish black hair, and usually wore tight, light-colored blue jeans and a jeans jacket over a T-shirt of some group like Depeche Mode. He was also a bit effeminate. But it turned out he was just into the New Wave genre of music and style—bands like Depeche Mode, The Cure, and The Smiths. I listened to them as well, since my musical taste varied from that to hip hop, rock, and even classical, but that didn't make *me* effeminate. Carlo grew less so over time due to our influence.

He was a smart guy. His comments were always insightful, and I enjoyed listening to his take on things. He was never argumentative and just wanted to understand things. This natural inquisitiveness made our conversations interesting, and although we didn't always agree, we moved on without holding a grudge.

Marty's house was a common spot for us to hang out because of his parents. They were like white parents… but Korean. Carlo, Ronnie, and Marty would smoke weed in the driveway, while Mitch and I would have Marty's older brother buy us beers to drink in Marty's room as we smoked Marlboro Lights. Marty's parents didn't mind. Sometimes, they would get on Marty about not going to class, and Marty would tell them he'd go the next day, but rarely did. Then a couple of weeks later, they'd get on him again. It was entertaining, and we'd give Marty a hard time about not going to school—even though we weren't doing any better.

Marty had a crazy side that would surface every so often, depending on the situation. He went out with a Korean girl, a UCLA student, who was staying at his place because she had problems at home. They went out for about a month, and it was weird having her around. She didn't know how to fit into our conversations, and would sit silently next to Marty most of the time, or they'd make out in the corner of the room while the rest of us just went on talking, smoking, and drinking.

He broke up with her when he caught her lying. She told him that she was meeting a friend, but it was another guy. He had his suspicions and followed her. He saw her get into a car with another guy, and make out with the dude. Then he started driving after them, chasing them on local streets until they were on the freeway. And there, in the middle of the day, on the 110 freeway, the oldest freeway in L.A., northbound underneath one of the three tunnels right before the I-5 freeway interchange, he got his car in front of them, stopped right in the middle of the freeway, got out, jumped on the guy's car hood, and started yelling at her, punching the windshield and telling the guy to get out of the car.

None of us were there for this. He nonchalantly told us all this while smoking a cigarette when we arrived at the house later and asked where his girlfriend was—after we saw a pile of her clothes and other items on the sidewalk.

The next year, Marty moved to Las Vegas without telling any of us. He stayed there for six months, selling random items, like day planners, to people walking on the Strip. Then he came back home with a thirtysomething-year-old white girlfriend who'd left her two kids in Las Vegas with her mother. Marty didn't just act crazy… he attracted it.

I went to see him the day after Ronnie called to tell me he was back in town. He was sitting in the middle of his room with his new girlfriend, wearing a cowboy hat and playing country music on his stereo. None of us had ever listened to country music, but here he was, telling us how he got into it when he was in Las Vegas, going to country western bars and line dancing.

This was in 1990. You didn't find Asians of *any* variety in country western bars.

In my head, I pictured him as the only Korean guy in the joint, line dancing with a big smile on his face and a cowboy hat on his head. I must've had an odd expression, because he laughed at me and said, "Yeah, I can't believe it either."

It was summer, and we would often hang out at Marty's place past midnight into the early morning. Sometimes Marty's mom would kick us out, saying we had school the next day. On weekends, we'd often spend the night, too high or too drunk to make it home. Then by late morning, we'd go to the plaza on Vermont and Olympic Boulevard, where there was a Korean-owned hamburger shop that sold teriyaki burritos. It was a fusion of bulgogi, beans, cheese, and white rice wrapped in a large flour tortilla. They were probably the first place to have a fusion of Korean and Mexican food.

Carlo and Marty got into an argument with Ronnie, Mitch, and me about how good a teriyaki burrito was before we started going there regularly. While eating this new fusion for the first time and letting the salsa and bulgogi blend in my mouth, wondering what other Mexican and Korean combinations would be so life-changing, I was listening to Carlo saying, "See, what did I tell you? My parents own a restaurant. I know what tastes good. Don't ever question my food choice again."

After that, Marty and Carlo became the last word on places we'd eat at.

Carlo had a car, a newer-model Toyota 4Runner, Mitch had a 1986 Toyota Corolla, and Marty had a 1978 Datsun B210. There was also the 1977 Toyota truck that Marty would alternate with his older brother. We all learned to drive in one or all four of those cars. Once, we even held a footrace against one of them.

Mitch, Arnie, and I were coming from Mitch's house, and we started arguing over who was faster, a person or a car. You might be asking, how *dumb* (or high) were these guys? We all understood that a car was faster than a person. The argument was over distance, and how long a person could hold a lead until the car took over. These were the days before Google and AI, so it had to be a first-person test. So we did what most guys would do back then: we pulled into a parking lot near the Capitol Records building on Vine Street in Hollywood, visible from the 101 Hollywood Freeway, and held a race with Mitch's 1986 Toyota Corolla… against Mitch himself.

He was fastest of the three of us, seeing as how Arnie was a walking wardrobe and I hated running. I was the driver, with Arnie in the passenger seat, hanging out the window to shout for the start of the race loud enough for Mitch to hear. The light pole that marked our finish line, after some arguing, was declared to be about fifty yards away.

"Okay… on 'go.' Ready… set… go!"

I stepped on the gas pedal like I was driving a Formula One race car and not a four-door family car. Mitch zipped way out ahead and the car barely seemed to be accelerating.

"Go faster!" Arnie shouted.

"My foot is on the pedal!"

"Shit, he's beating us."

"That's because you're wearing a week's worth of clothes, Arnie!"

Mitch beat us to the pole. I told him that was only because of Arnie weighing the Toyota down. I wanted a rematch *without* a passenger. Mitch was game. We raced again. He won again.

Arnie was just starting to suggest that we remove the spare tire when Mitch cut him off.

"Fuck that! I'm not running again!"

"C'mon, Mitch, it was close," Arnie insisted.

It wasn't really that close. Arnie just enjoyed watching Mitch run and pant to the point of exhaustion just to prove he was right. But now Mitch was too tired and the suggestion of a third attempt was pissing him off.

Oh well. We left the parking lot laughing over what morons we must've looked like from the freeway, or to anyone looking out from the Capitol Building.

Mitch's Toyota was the same car we would ride out into a smoke-filled, chaotic scenario in just three short years.

I miss that Corolla.

CHAPTER TWELVE

Someone thought it would be a good idea to open a nightclub for sixteen- to twenty-year-old kids in the city of Pasadena. The club was called Marilyn's, and it was open on Saturday evening. We'd go there occasionally, but there was always a possibility that a fight would occur, either inside the club or out in the parking lot.

One Saturday night, we got into a fight with another group at a gas station a few blocks north of the nightclub on Lake Avenue. Four carloads of guys followed us after a few of their guys had verbal exchanges with us in the club's parking lot. We were with a larger group of about twenty, so nothing happened… at least not there.

That big group separated and planned to meet at someone's house later that evening. Mitch, Marty, Ronnie, Carlo, rode with me and my girlfriend. We were in the car my father bought for me in the fall of 1989—a brand-new Hyundai Sonata. This was the first year the model came out, and a patriotic buy, according to him, to support the first Korean car company in America. Carlo was riding in the back seat, and on the way to the club, he gave me pointers on how to scan all the mirrors as I drove on the freeway for the first time—the 110 freeway going north, where it ended at the edge of Pasadena.

We stopped at a gas station, and while I was pumping gas, I heard Ronnie say, “Looks like they followed us.”

There were about ten or twelve of them. A large Hispanic guy walked up to me and asked, “Who’s the guy with the smart mouth?” He was referring to me.

I had told them in the club’s parking lot to “take a walk” since they were outnumbered, and no one came to the club intentionally to fight. They didn’t appreciate my remarks. We recognized one of them from a rival crew, STS. To make things even more fun, it was a guy my girlfriend had dated in the past.

I hadn’t finished filling the Hyundai’s gas tank, and it didn’t seem like I was going to.

“You talking about me?” I asked the guy.

“Hey, man, you got a big mouth.”

“So, what are you—”

I was going to finish the sentence with “going to do about it” but those words never made it out of my mouth. He threw a punch that connected with my jaw.

I honestly thought we were going to verbally go back and forth a bit more first, but given how badly they outnumbered us, and the fact that in the parking lot earlier we'd outnumbered them, I wasn't too surprised once the fists began to fly.

My reaction was instantaneous. I grabbed his throat and punched him under his right eye, hitting his cheekbone, and then we were both throwing and taking punches. Fists were flying as we moved from the car that was being pumped to the open area in the middle of the gas station.

It happened fast. One of his friends, another big Hispanic guy, joined the melee and then I was dealing with two guys who were both twice my size, but I didn't care. I was moving, connecting, and I could see the redness build on the first Hispanic guy's face while punching the second guy. I moved to get a bit of space between me and the first guy.

Then the second guy landed a punch on the back of my head, and a moment later, I was on my back looking up at the ceiling of the gas station carport as the two guys ran back to their car.

I hadn't been the only one fighting. All of us were taking on two to three guys apiece. We weren't making it easy, even though we were outnumbered. The fight probably lasted only a minute or two; the STS guys probably thought our other friends weren't that far behind us.

Turned out, that was true.

Shortly after the gas station cleared, two carloads of our other friends arrived. They quickly rode out looking for them, but I knew they wouldn't find them. We were close to the freeway, and they'd probably hopped on it right after the fight.

That following week, my girlfriend told her brother what happened, and her brother attempted to set up a one-on-one fight between me and her ex-boyfriend, but the guy declined. I suppose it was a surprise to him that I knew a *veterano* (Spanish for "veteran," an older member) or OG (original gangster) from his crew, in addition to my fighting two of the biggest guys in his group that night.

The gas station was Carlo's first time getting into a fight, and something changed in him that night. He experienced what it feels like to have a group of guys fight with you. It's a unique, shared, unforgettable experience and helps build camaraderie among men. I think that night set the stage for his gradual transformation later. It gave him a taste of what it's like running with a bunch of rough guys whose second language was violence—a far cry from the life his parents raised him in.

We all went to Marty's house afterward to recount what happened to each of us—how many punches we got in, and how the one punch I took from the heavyset Hispanic guy set off a chain reaction. Ronnie had three guys he was fighting, hitting one then getting hit by the other two. He mentioned the math was all wrong for him; for every punch he threw, he'd receive two in return.

One guy grabbed Marty's jacket by the shoulders with two hands and was trying to spin him around like a helicopter, which inadvertently worked in Marty's favor. While the other guy waited for his chance to punch Marty, Marty was able to get in several punches on the guy trying to spin him. Marty was a rounder and more heavyset guy than me. He should have been the one fighting the big Hispanic dudes who were double-teaming me! Unfortunately, you don't get to pick your opponents in these situations; you get what comes at you. I suppose that's life sometimes. You want to fight the two smaller Asian guys, but get stuck with the two biggest Mexicans instead.

Mitch said he protected my new Hyundai from a trash can that was knocked toward the car after I got punched. Ronnie recounted how he felt like a pinball getting bounced between guys, punching one then getting punched by a second guy, punching back then getting punched by a third guy.

Carlo went ballistic in the fight, yelling, "Fuck you, come get it, motherfucker!"

During the melee, I didn't hear him. I had tunnel vision, hearing and dealing only with the two guys who easily outweighed me. But in our post-fight talk, I learned that Carlo charged at two guys even though he'd never fought before.

I think every man, to a certain extent, knows what a punch is, and tries his best to emulate it during a fight—a balled-up fist hurled at your target. That was what happened: he got in several punches, took a few punches, and then it was all over as the other guys ran toward their cars.

After recounting what happened during the fight got old, we turned to making fun of each other. Marty said the two Hispanic guys should've just sat on me. Marty had a black smudge mark on the left side of his forehead, and Ronnie remarked how Marty's opponent had dirty hands—that he probably worked as a mechanic and didn't wash his hands after using the bathroom either, so Ronnie claimed Marty probably got hit with "penis hands." And everyone teased Mitch for having lost his fight with a trash can.

I appreciated that he protected my car, but I also would've been fine with a couple of dents in the car as a reminder of the occasion. And even though we teased Mitch, I never questioned his willingness to "get down" with things that needed to happen and never be spoken about after. It was what I recognized in his voice when he called me a few years later asking me to ride out with him that week. Something we would do together and never talk about because it was "one of those things."

Carlo wasn't as jovial as the rest of us for the remainder of the night. He was reserved, and I knew the fight was somewhat of a shock to him, as was his own reaction to it. That didn't stop us, though. We laughed about it into the early morning before Marty's mom, bleary-eyed and annoyed, kicked us out of the house for being loud and told us to go home.

CHAPTER THIRTEEN

When Mitch and Arnie weren't off "fishnapping," we'd walk around Melrose Avenue, occupying ourselves with the different shops. This was before the 1990s TV series called *Melrose Place*, where young twentysomethings lived in an apartment complex together doing life and work. In the mid to late '80s, Melrose Avenue was full of shops that catered to the New Wave music genre and carried the Boy London brand or Euro type of clothing—baggy shirts with tight pants. It never appealed to me since I thought it made you look gay, even if you weren't.

Parking was always on the street with a meter that took quarters, dimes, and nickels. It took about $1.50 to park for an hour and a half, which was fairly expensive when all you're given is five dollars for the day.

Someone showed Mitch and Arnie a way to maximize the time on the meter with a penny. I remember the first time they did it. We found an open spot with a meter. I had two quarters and said we could probably exchange a dollar bill for coins at one of the shops. But Mitch said, “Don’t bother. Let me show you something cool.”

He took a penny from the coin tray and started filing it down on the concrete. “You want to get to the tip of Lincoln’s head,” he said as he kept filing.

After he got tired, he passed the penny to Arnie, who continued filing the penny. When it was reduced to a certain size, the rounded penny was noticeably straight on one side. They inserted it into the dime slot and turned the dial. It maxed out the time.

It was ingenious, and I liked it. This allowed us to park on Melrose anytime. The trick reminded me of something I used to do three years earlier, riding the bus with Tim and Patrick.

The RTD buses—before Los Angeles County renamed them Metro buses—had a clear glass deposit box to drop your money into. Then the bus driver flipped a lever, which dropped the money into a metal container beneath the deposit box. It was $1.00 for the ride and $1.25 for a transfer ticket to catch another bus or use it for the return ride back.

Tim and Patrick would cut a dollar in half, fold a penny into it so it added a bit of weight, and drop that into the box, along with a quarter for the transfer.

Bus drivers would quickly flip the lever to drop the money into the holding box below without a second thought. Eventually, though, they must have been tipped off by whoever counted the money. They started to eyeball the dollar, and then us when what we put in didn't look quite believable. Once, Tim was caught red-handed and got into a heated argument with a big black male bus driver.

"That shit's a ripped-in-half dollar bill!"

"What? No, man, that's a dollar. What are you talking about?"

It was only a couple of years later they switched to the electronic machines that required an unfolded bill to be inserted, but I was so close to having my license that I didn't care.

The summer came and went pretty fast, and with my new car, we were even more mobile. In the fall, we spent our time "Wonka Tonkwa-ing." The term came from a TV commercial for Sprite; in it, a couple was looking for a place on a map called Wonka Tonkwa, which was just a sign in the middle of nowhere. So we did the same, picking a random local spot by the beach or around the Malibu canyons and driving out there at night, taking La Tuna Canyon from the valley and making our way to Malibu. At that hour, we had to be careful not to drive over the rabbits that kept crossing the road. We were kids with too much time on our hands, just doing things to entertain ourselves.

Only one of us went to school in the fall. It was Marty. Everyone else had dropped out. Carlo quit going to Valley College, and by the holidays, his parents were on him about it, but he was having too much fun wasting time with us. Up to that point, he had done everything his parents asked him to do, following their plan. But now, he was doing what *he* wanted to do, which was smoke weed, hang out with friends, and do pointless stuff like Wonka Tonkwa-ing.

Carlo, Ronnie, and Perry were potheads and would meet up around noon before everyone else met up with them at Marty's place by four or four thirty.

This lasted about one to two months before Marty stopped going to school, too. I guess there was no one to hang out with at school, and sitting in class knowing that your friends were having fun and waiting for you probably didn't help. Since Marty, Ronnie, and Carlo lived close by, they were frequently together. Mitch, Arnie, and I were similarly close to each other and hung out together before everyone would meet up.

The fall routine was similar to the summer before I got my car. Mitch would pick me up at seven thirty a.m., or I would go and get him with my brand-new car, then we'd get to Arnie's place and yell at his window while waiting fifteen to twenty minutes for him, occasionally threatening to leave. Once he'd layered on enough clothing to hold his own personal garage sale, we'd go to a cafe across the street from Los Angeles City College (LACC), get breakfast, and then spend the rest of our money at one of the two arcades, playing video games.

When Marty stopped going to classes, he'd meet us at the arcade, then we'd all go to his place by nine thirty or ten a.m. to take a nap or hang out while we smoked cigarettes in his room, dialing a phone number called "the Party Line."

The Party Line was a phone number to conference call with random people. It's comparable to a chat room but with voice, and it was chaotic. It was a place where you could meet girls or argue with guys to impress the girls. Ronnie and Carlo spent the most time on it— sometimes they were on the phone until two or three in the morning—and the rest of us were entertained by their banter and arguments.

You had no idea how anyone looked on the Party Line, but Ronnie had a saying: "The cuter the girl sounds, the fatter she is." He was right. On more than several occasions when they actually followed through with meeting one of the girls in person who sounded really hot on the phone, she was fat. Maybe it was just them. Later, it became common practice for them to have a meetup someplace that was a highly visible public setting and stay anonymous. They met and left a lot of girls hanging at the laundromat.

We had too much time on our hands. It would lead to more trouble.

CHAPTER FOURTEEN

Perry was older than us by a few years and worked in the shoe department of the May Company department store, which later became Robinsons-May. When he'd show up in the evening, Ronnie would call him "Al Bundy," after the character from the show *Married with Children* who also sold shoes. Perry didn't care. Out of all of us, he was the only one who had a job… and money. So he took it all in stride, flashing a wad of twenty-dollar bills in front of us and smiling. Most of the time, he'd buy the group dinner; Perry was always generous like that.

I met Perry in summer school at Hollywood High, a year after I met Ronnie. I initiated Perry into our crew, and he was one of our best fighters. He was Thai, with a thin, muscular build, and a little shorter than my 5'10".

I still remember when he was "jumped in"—a gang initiation where you fought multiple guys for a certain amount of time. Me and two others were maneuvering around him to sandwich and punch him, but he kept evading us and we hardly landed anything on him. He kept deflecting and parrying the punches, a technique he'd learned in the Muay Thai (Thai kickboxing) training that his parents had sent him to when he was younger. By the time the two minutes were up, I think the three of us had landed only two or three punches. It was too bad he'd missed the fight at the gas station; he was working that night and regretted not being there.

Perry lived in Hollywood proper, on Franklin Avenue and Gower Street, right next to the freeway overpass. I liked his parents, especially his mom. During the time I was at odds with my father, I'd sometimes stay with them. She'd call my father to let him know where I was even though they never met and she didn't know him. God bless her.

Perry's younger brother, Charley, was about three years younger than Perry and would talk down to Perry whenever he was home and one of us was around. "You fucking loser wannabe gangster. Does Tony know what a loser you are?" was a typical comment, or maybe: "You're such a dumbass wannabe gangster, go to college, you loser. Why does Tony hang out with you? Why do you hang out with him, Tony?"

Perry told me that when they lived in Thailand prior to coming to America, Charley was possessed by an evil spirit, and his parents took him to a Buddhist temple to have it exorcised. Because of that, Perry tolerated how Charley talked to him in front of us. He felt bad for Charley and would always overlook his comments or laugh them off. He also said that when it was just the two of them, Charley wouldn't talk that way. He was just trying to impress me and the other guys when we were around.

Perry's dad had an internal decibel meter that was broken or turned off, because the first time I was over at his place and Perry's dad spoke to him, I thought he was in trouble and I was about to leave.

"Dude, is your dad mad at you? I'll get going."

"What? No, man. He just said, 'Don't forget to take out the trash before you leave.'"

"You're kidding. That's what he said? I thought he was yelling at you."

"That's just the way he talks."

I laughed. "Damn, I thought he was pissed at you. Let me know when you're *actually* in trouble. I'll want to hear him *then*."

"Shut up, man."

When Ronnie and I were at Perry's place, we'd mimic Charley—insulting Perry the way he did—or we'd pretend to be Perry's dad, yelling at Perry like his father, in our pretend Thai.

Perry was a good friend… until he met a girl. After that, he no longer came around or picked up calls, and he was never at home. His disappearing act was better than any magician's, and it was something the rest of us would talk about, especially Ronnie, since Perry was supposed to be Ronnie's ride until he got his own car.

There was one incident when Perry was going to pick up Ronnie to hang out—without Perry's girlfriend for a change—but Perry never showed up. He didn't call and left Ronnie waiting all day. When Perry did call him—the *next* day—he was apologetic. But Ronnie knew from then on that Perry was a different guy when he had a girl. Perry's shortcoming was getting so wrapped up with a girl that he neglected his friends.

I still loved the guy. His driving skills were second to none, having lost undercover officers tailing us on multiple occasions during the evenings when we were visiting friends whose homes were being staked out by LAPD. He'd saved my life more than once as we were getting shot at.

On one occasion, he prevented me from taking my own life after a really bad argument with my father. He overheard my father yell, "You killed your mother!"

Without Perry, I wouldn't be here. I still owe him a debt of gratitude that he tells me has long been repaid.

No, it hasn't, Perry. You're always too kind and generous, my friend.

CHAPTER FIFTEEN

Of the members in the group, I'd known Ronnie the longest. He was two years older than me, and we met through a mutual friend, Ricky, who I met through Patrick. Ricky was a member of BNG and would later become one of the founders of TGP. Ronnie and I met at Arby's, a fast-food roast beef restaurant, across the street from Hollywood High. That place has since been replaced with condominiums and retail shops.

When Ronnie told me that he was skipping school, I gave him my key and told him that he could hang out at my house during school hours. Since my father owned a market, our apartment wasn't always empty. It was always stocked with Cup O' Noodles and Squirt soda. He would smoke and watch TV until I came home.

He still brings those times up, to this day. Even at his wedding, he recounted how we met and my telling him right off that he could hang out at my place. I suppose it still blows his mind that someone he had just met would say, "Hey, you can hang out at my place, totally unsupervised, until I get home."

Ronnie told me that the first day he went to my apartment he went inside cautiously, smoked some cigarettes, and listened to a CD on our CD player. (At the time, CDs were a new medium replacing cassette tapes, and no one he knew had a CD player yet.) Back then, I only had the first CD I'd bought—*Standing on a Beach* by the Cure—and he played it through the morning and into the afternoon. That was how our friendship started.

When Ronnie had problems at home, he would run away and stay at a halfway house for teen runaways a couple of blocks north of Hollywood Boulevard in the evening. He'd still stay at my place during the day. I would've been at my house with him during that time, except for the fact that I had to make an effort to stay in school. I had already been kicked out of Van Nuys High and was close to getting kicked out of North Hollywood High. I wanted to go to Hollywood High, the school I was supposed to go to in the first place, but my father was against it, knowing that most of the friends that I got into trouble with were there.

One day, my father came home unexpectedly during the school day, and Ronnie got busted. The funny thing was, he wasn't alone. There were about fifteen other kids there too. Let me unpack this disaster, because we still laugh about it today:

An ex-girlfriend introduced me to one of her friends, and we started talking on the phone. This was before email and the internet, so she physically mailed me a picture of herself, which took a few days to arrive. She looked pretty in the picture, so we kept talking and made plans to meet. But, the ex-girlfriend started talking to one of my friends, and the next thing I knew, a simple meet-up between the girl and me ended up becoming a party at my apartment during school hours.

The plan was for everyone to be there by noon, and for me to join them after school at three. Ronnie told me the place was *packed*. People were smoking, someone brought some beers, and by one, the party was already gaining momentum.

It was one thirty when Ronnie heard a key slide into the lock.

Then the door opened, and there, within the doorframe, stood my father, looking at a pack of teenagers in his apartment, smoking, drinking, and playing music.

The mood changed so fast. Several of the guys who were smoking put out their cigarettes and started coughing, trying not to exhale their smoke in front of my father.

Without saying a word, my father walked across the apartment, shut off the stereo, turned around, and calmly asked, "What are you all doing here? Where is my son?"

The girls—the one I was going to meet, my ex-girlfriend, and a few others—immediately started crying. Everyone was in trouble and they knew it. No one knew what to do.

So Ronnie spoke up. "Tony's not here. He's in school, sir."

This was how Ronnie met my father for the first time.

"You shouldn't be here. You should all be in school," my father stated in an even tone.

And that was all he needed to say. Everyone quickly started making their way to the door.

"Who has a key to my apartment?" my father asked.

Both Ronnie and Ricky voluntarily gave up their copies of the key. And they, along with several other people, apologized as they left, which I thought was classy of them.

I got off the bus at Hollywood and Highland after an hour-and-a-half bus ride from North Hollywood High expecting to party. Instead, I ran into three of the guys at the McDonald's.

"What the…what are you guys doing here?"

"Your dad showed up."

"What?!"

"Yeah, man, your dad came home."

Of all the days for him to check up on me, it *had* to be the day I was going to meet this girl that I'd been talking to on the phone for a couple of weeks. There would be no coming back from that. The disappointment hit hard, and I was already coming up with excuses and lies to avoid getting into trouble with him later in the evening. They told me what happened and how everyone went in different directions afterward. Ronnie, Ricky, and a few of the guys went with my ex and her friend toward Silverlake, near another high school called Marshall High, while the rest went back to Hollywood High.

That wasn't the end of it, either. Ronnie, Ricky, and the girls stopped by a supermarket in the area, and undercover LAPD caught the girls outside for truancy. Ronnie and Ricky saw the girls get escorted into the back of an unmarked squad car and driven off, presumably back to their school. I didn't hear from either of them after that; they were probably punished by their parents. They were "good girls" from a private Catholic girls' school, and their parents probably took away their privileges, including using the phone.

That evening when my father came back home from work, he pretended like nothing happened, and I followed along. He asked me if I went to school, and I told him I did. That was it. I think he was shocked at what he'd opened the door to that afternoon, never imagining he'd see a bunch of teenagers having a party in his apartment. Sometimes I wish I had been there to see the expression on his face, even though it would've meant getting into so much trouble. Part of me thought it would've been worth it.

After that, I never had a large group at the apartment without being there myself.

A few months later, I got kicked out of North Hollywood High for excessive absences. Exasperated, my father exclaimed, "You said you were going to school!"

"I did," I replied. "I just didn't go to class."

The smartass comment resulted in a smack on top of my head from his keychain.

Later, when I told Ronnie about the comment and getting hit with the keychain, he laughed and said I was lucky that was all I'd received after that party, and after getting kicked out of my second high school.

In hindsight, he was correct. I would need more than getting hit by a keychain to pull up from the downward spiral I was in. But I was having too much fun with Ronnie to even care.

CHAPTER SIXTEEN

Ronnie was the youngest of six, and the rest were girls. His father insisted on having kids until he got a boy; his wish was granted on the sixth try. Being the youngest and the only boy, Ronnie had the privilege of being pampered by his mom and sisters. Whenever I'd visit, his sisters were always nice to me, which made me feel bad that we'd get into trouble or skip school together. They resented me at times for that, but I redeemed myself by convincing Ronnie to go to college.

That was later, in the summer of 1993, a year after the riots. We were sitting and eating at Pink's Hot Dog near Melrose Avenue, and I gave him facts to encourage him to pursue a college degree. We didn't come from rich families, and college was the only opportunity available to us to get into higher-paying professions. I was already finishing up my general education classes at LACC and getting ready to transfer to the University of Southern California. Our conversation touched something within him, and he enrolled in LACC. After two years, he transferred to CSU-Northridge, where he graduated with a bachelor's degree in sociology. He also met his wife there, and they went on to have a beautiful daughter together.

But from the winter of 1989 until the following summer, we were generally all hanging out at Marty's. And as with most friendships between young men, whenever women are introduced to the group… it complicates things.

I already had a girlfriend. Arnie's girlfriend was pregnant, which would later lead to friction with her, once his daughter was born. But two new girls entered our lives during that period—two girls who were cousins. And Mitch, Marty, Carlo, Perry, and Ronnie were all vying for one or the other.

The older cousin, Pam, liked Ronnie, although she didn't tell him that until several months later, when she was about to move to Colorado. After she moved, Ronnie and Carlo drove to Colorado for a church retreat that Carlo was a part of, with loose plans to see Pam if there was time. They took turns driving and smoking weed all the way there. They stopped in Las Vegas, got drunk, then drove straight to Colorado through a blizzard. It was snowing so much, they could hardly see thirty feet in front of them. They were so high at a certain point that they started seeing people just standing on the side of the highway late in the evening looking at their car drive by. They weren't sure if the people were real or if the two of them were sharing a hallucination.

The church organization wasn't aware that Ronnie was with Carlo. Actually, I'm sure they weren't aware about a lot of things when it came to Carlo. Anyway, Ronnie stayed in Carlo's Toyota 4Runner the first night, leaving it running so he didn't freeze to death. Carlo didn't say anything because he didn't want to get in trouble, since Ronnie didn't tell his parents that he was going to cross several state lines.

On the second night, the pastor found out that Ronnie was staying in the 4Runner, so he invited him to stay with everyone else at the retreat. They both stayed there, praying, crying, singing, eating, and socializing. Ronnie said they were the nicest people he'd ever met, and he really gave being a Christian a thought. I asked him why he didn't follow through, and he said it was probably because the drive home was the same as the drive there. Stoned and dazed—how they drove to Colorado was how they returned to California.

They never did end up seeing Pam.

It was Alyssa, the younger cousin, who caused a rift in our group, because both Perry and Mitch liked her. Perry was the one who ended up with her, and because of that, he was no longer in the picture after a while. When he was around, Mitch didn't want to hang with him because he still felt rejected and upset over Alyssa.

The situation forced all of us to pick a side, though we tried to bridge the growing gap; two distinct groups developed. Mitch, Arnie, and I formed one group, while Ronnie, Marty, and Carlo formed the other.

Shortly after that, Ronnie's parents sent him to live with his married oldest sister in Chino Hills, because all he did was smoke weed. His mother and father thought taking him out of his current environment would be a good thing. That was when Marty went to Las Vegas to go country western without telling anyone.

Without Ronnie around, Carlo started to reconnect with friends from junior high school, friends who were now the founders that formed a new Salvadoran gang called Mara Salvatrucha, or MS for short. Translated into English it meant "street smart Salvadorans."

They would later align themselves with the Mexican Mafia and add the number 13 to become MS13.

With the new friend group came a new style for Carlo. Gone were the light-blue faded jeans, T-shirt, and denim jacket; instead, he wore white T-shirts with oversized dark blue jeans, and Nike Cortez. His long, curlyish black hair was now cut short and slicked back. He was indistinguishable from the other MS members. His attitude also changed. During the time he drove to Colorado with Ronnie, he was religious, with talks about God.

I only knew Bible stories and not the application of living through the words in the Bible, but at times, Carlo would lecture or evangelize, and he got upset with Ronnie when he slept with Pam before she left for Colorado, stating that sex outside marriage was something God frowned on. Ronnie was put off by Carlo after that, and they had a weird vibe for a day before they got over it. It was unlike Carlo or Ronnie to hold a grudge. I suppose some sins were more serious to him than others. Sleeping out of wedlock was his trigger while getting high was "not that bad." Up until we met him, I don't think he ever slept with a girl, so he saw it as something sacred between a husband and wife. But if our level of mischief and activity was a gateway, his new friends would take him to another level to the point that he would later be charged and convicted of manslaughter of a homeless guy.

Carlo's older brother, who was going into the LAPD, had a huge problem with Carlo and his friends from the past. It got so bad that Carlo and his older brother physically fought in their living room one day. After that, Carlo left home for a while and lived with friends. He would go from one couch to another in the evenings, getting high and drunk. In the day, he was getting into trouble. He still kept in touch with Ronnie and Marty throughout that time. And when he was incarcerated for his affiliations and some petty crimes, Ronnie and Marty rode with Carlo's then-girlfriend to visit him at Peter J. Pitchess Detention Center, commonly known as "Wayside" by law enforcement and those incarcerated.

The girlfriend drove Carlo's Toyota 4Runner, and the guys told me it was one of the scariest drives ever—and this was coming from Ronnie, who shared that weed-fueled trip through the Colorado blizzard with Carlo. She was high and distracted, talking to both Marty and Ronnie while drifting between lanes on the freeway. For the return trip, one of the guys drove instead, under the pretense that she should take a break since it had been a long drive getting there. She obliged, and both Ronnie and Marty were relieved.

When they met Carlo at Wayside, they were shocked at how much he had transformed in the months since they'd seen each other last—not just physically, but in his "fuck this and everyone" attitude. His mom visited him several days before, crying at the visitors' window as he stood there expressionless, telling her it was going to be all right despite the bruises, cuts, and scrapes on his face. The most difficult visits for Ronnie and Marty were when they would take Carlo's mom with them. She'd cry all the way there and on the way back.

Back then, MS wasn't integrated into the Los Angeles prison system like it is today. So like any new group, they were pressed by the other groups, especially the Mexicans, who had a long-established history in the L.A. prison system. With the Mexicans, it was fairly simple: no matter what neighborhood or "hood" you represented, you fell under the larger umbrella of the Mexican Mafia, or La Eme. Your past issues with rivals no longer held as much weight, and you were now part of a much larger organization until you got out. And once you were involved in the prison system hierarchy, it followed you when you left.

The Salvadorans didn't have that system when they entered prison, and had to fight to carve out their place. It didn't make things easier that their main rival, 18th Street, was already entrenched and had a lot of influence. The result was that Carlo fought almost daily. Being taller and built bigger than most Hispanics, he had a constant target on his back, and narrowly avoided getting stabbed several times in different encounters.

Life outside prison was better for Carlo, unless LAPD was involved. They knew how to take advantage of the rivalry between gangs. They'd employ dirty tactics like picking up a member from a rival gang and dropping him off deep in enemy territory while yelling his gang affiliations to bring attention to the drop-off. It was like dropping a piece of meat within a school of piranhas. That was why every gangster in Los Angeles back then knew that the largest and most organized gang was LAPD.

The current LAPD of 2025 is a shadow of its former self—full of report takers, paycheck/pension collectors, and apathetic, out-of-shape bodies. The physical requirements for it have been lowered, too; many of the current officers, both men and women, would never have qualified under the late 1980s and early 1990s standards. Those former officers are discouraging their children from joining the force, because it's been politicized to focus on LGBTQ and DEI, which rewards people based on the current social hierarchy of female, gay, trans, black, whatever… instead of physical strength, agility, mental clarity, and moral integrity. The ultimate thanks for this goes to the Democrat supermajority city leaders with the foresight to support defunding the police, which will also reduce crime, since police always end up entangled with crime.

"No police, no crime" is the kind of forward-thinking leadership we get. From my experience, that's not how it has ever worked, especially during the riots.

All that said, the LAPD from the past was hardly spotless. They were, after all, responsible for the biggest police corruption scandal in US history, when in 1998, Officer Rafael Pérez became an informant after getting caught taking cocaine that was being held as evidence—and then implicated more than seventy officers, which in turn overturned previous criminal convictions. The movie *Training Day* drew on the Rampart era.

Gangs were fully aware of this corruption in CRASH during the early '90s, because many were on the receiving end of the corrupt officers, and a few were collaborators with LAPD. Everyone was a gangster in the 1990s, even the cops.

Carlo relayed an incident when he was with seven or eight of his friends at someone's house, and the LAPD raided. The police had everyone lie face down in a bedroom with their hands clasped behind their backs, then turned off the lights—and a couple of the officers urinated on them in the dark.

Why do this to them but not their rivals? Because MS was the only gang that would shoot at LAPD.

That blatant disregard and disrespect made them angry. Many of the young men who left El Salvador during the height of its civil war took with them a deep suspicion of law enforcement, given the corruption in that country. They brought a new level of violence to the streets of L.A. and the San Fernando Valley, where many of them were bused to Grant High School, under the Los Angeles Unified School District's Magnet Program. The idea was to send urban kids to the suburbs with the goal of providing a better learning opportunity and to diversify the school. But it's like the saying I heard growing up: "You can take the thug out of the streets, but you can't take the streets out of the thug."

The Salvadorans fighting their civil war imported some of their tactics to L.A., making gang warfare evolve on the streets. We heard rumors of MS using grenades, with one story of how they lobbed one at another gang hanging out in an alley. The couple of Salvadorans we knew confirmed the rumors, since they had older brothers and uncles connected to their friends in El Salvador. Molotov cocktails were also modified to create homemade napalm using common items, and having that thrown at rivals accompanied by gunfire was a destructive element. We were entering a new era of gang warfare in Los Angeles.

Eventually, Carlo was released and went home. But while his mother was still heartbroken with Carlo's direction in life and wanted to rehabilitate him, his father and older brother didn't want him around. That might sound harsh, but given the violence that followed him—and more importantly, the influence it was having on his younger brother, I can see why they did it. Ronnie told me that the week before Carlo was kicked out of the house, Carlo's younger brother was emulating Carlo's hairstyle and had changed his wardrobe, wearing baggier clothes. He was even starting to talk and sound like Carlo.

As Carlo went deeper into MS, it became harder for Ronnie and Marty to keep in touch with him. When Carlo had been in prison, he'd collect-call them. (For those too young to know what that means, the receiver of the call paid for it—a common way to make a call from prison.) But once he was on the outside, and not staying in one place, staying in touch was harder. This was a time long before cell phones.

People could disappear, and you wouldn't run into them again except by chance. Or maybe, in the case of Carlo… fate.

CHAPTER SEVENTEEN

By early 1992, we had pretty much gone our separate ways and were all doing our own thing. I wasn't in contact with Ronnie and Perry, but I knew what the others were up to. Marty was working at his parents' swap meet, along with his older brother; Mitch was working at an office supply retailer; Arnie was a new father, figuring out life with his baby; and Carlo was moving up in MS.

And me? I was nineteen years old and working as a car salesman at a Nissan dealership in Alhambra, a small city east of Downtown L.A. It was my first sales job, and I was pretty good at talking to people. Since I really liked the new Nissan Maxima, that became the running joke at the dealership: Tony was going to sell everyone a Maxima regardless of their budget.

I was working as much as I could, and I didn't hang out with anyone except my girlfriend. Weekends were the best time to work, as there was a lot of foot traffic, so that prevented me from drinking and staying out late. Plus, the management liked me, a young kid who became the top salesperson the second month he was there. I couldn't hold on to that title, though, no matter how hard I tried. There was a woman who just *dominated* and held the top spot month after month. It turned out that was because she was sleeping with the general sales manager. He'd give her practically closed sales from people who happened to call or walk into the dealership looking for him. They got married several years later and had a girl.

It was while I was working at the dealership that the video of Rodney King getting beaten by LAPD went public. Rodney King took the LAPD on a chase through L.A. and ended up getting beat like he owed somebody money.

It shocked everyone. Video camcorders were a new technology, and capturing moments like this was a novelty, unlike today with cell phones. Camcorders were large and bulky, about the size of a small ice cooler, so getting video was purposeful, not on-the-fly like whipping out your cell phone. People hadn't seen videos like this before.

Those of us who had a background on the streets in L.A. and dealt with LAPD knew why they were beating Rodney King. Few things upset the LAPD of the 1990s more than having to chase someone down, whether on foot or in the car.

Back then, we knew that if you ran and got caught, there was going to be a "leave no mark" beating at the station, possibly involving baton strikes to the abdomen. Or if they were pissed enough, you'd get a bruised lip and a black eye from "running into a wall" or "tripping over your untied shoelaces."

This video was the catalyst that started the L.A. Riots that would have me going out to help Mitch and other Koreans.

At the time, the video looked brutal and senseless; everyone was appalled at the imagery. After thirty-plus years of comparing how mainstream corporate media reports, I see it now as an early example of lying by omission, which sadly has become the norm.

Even at nineteen years old, while my emotions on the beating were fired up, I knew there had to be *something* that led up to the incident. LAPD didn't pull King out of the car and decide to just "beat a nigga" for the fun of it that night.

While the media showed the world only the beating, the court system, and more importantly, the jury, were privileged to see the full video and hear the testimony of the two passengers that were with King and were also arrested. The media simply glossed over that information along with the fact the chase went from the highway to the street.

King was inebriated and impaired, having been drinking throughout the night. He also had taken "dust" (angel dust,

PCP) and been smoking weed. The man's mental acuity and response were dulled or deadened, and so was any pain he felt that night. King was going to weather the beating as if he was getting hit with pipe insulation instead of a baton—of course, the next morning would be another matter; he would certainly feel the beating after he woke up and the high was gone.

So the LAPD were responding with force, but it was a force they felt was necessary to get any sort of compliance from a drugged-out man who behaved as though he were impervious to physical subduing.

It was the timing of this video as much as the contents itself that sparked the fire that would become the L.A. Riots. When news channels began to air the footage, the black community was already contending with the death of Latasha Harlins.

Harlins was a fourteen-year-old black teen girl who was shot in the back of the head after a physical confrontation with an elderly Korean woman, Soon Ja Du, who was working the cash register at a market similar to my family's. Harlins started the altercation after she had been accused of attempting to steal orange juice. When Harlins turned to leave after battering the old woman, Soon Ja retrieved a revolver from under the counter and shot her.

Soon Ja stated that she had never been beaten like that before and was in a state of fear and panic when she shot

Latasha. The jury and judge found the circumstances extraordinary and tragic, sentencing Soon Ja to probation for involuntary manslaughter. I saw snippets of it on TV and overheard my father talking to his friends, and people on both cultural sides were upset.

Was the use of force necessary?

After thirty years, the verdict is what it is and everything else is an opinion. In my opinion, until you've worked behind a cash register for at least a month in an inner city neighborhood that is predominately black, you have no valid opinion or idea of what you're talking about.

Working in my father's markets in Boyle Heights and Huntington Park, we hardly saw black customers. There were more blacks at the Huntington Park market than Boyle Heights because the surrounding cities in Boyle Heights were Latino while Huntington Park borders South Los Angeles. For the most part, people were generally cool or low key. They would come in, find what they needed, come to the register, pay for their items then leave.

But every so often, you get a knucklehead, be it a man or woman. Most of the time, they were black. Some readers might not like me saying that, but that was what I experienced. These are black people that annoy everyone, even other black people.

“How much is this? What? Man, that’s expensive, it’s cheaper over at…”

It was people incapable of just shrugging their shoulders and paying the price, or going wherever they thought they could find it cheaper.

When this would happen, I was already mentally geared up for a verbal back and forth about some little thing this individual was going to turn into a big thing. Like what brands we kept in stock, as if we could put every product in existence on the shelves.

“You guys don’t carry my favorite brand? What the fuck?”

Whenever one of those customers visited, my father would stop whatever he was doing and just stand and watch them.

Does that seem racist?

It wasn’t. Race had nothing to do with it—it was identifying a certain personality type. My father simply developed habits from repeated, predictable encounters. Sometimes it would end without trouble.

Other times, it would take a thirteen-year-old Korean kid telling them, “Hey, this is Huntington Park; South Central is that way. Better get there before the sun goes down.”

“What? The fuck did you say, kid?” They would turn toward me with a scowl on their face and that glint of violence

I could see in their eye because knuckleheads only respect violence.

"Oh, this is also a Florencia 13 neighborhood."

They would pause and consider the implications of *that* fact, then leave while giving me a stinky look. I didn't care.

Similarly, in the Rodney King case, the police officers were acquitted, having convinced a jury that their actions, while extreme-looking in the video, were necessary due to King's reckless state of intoxication, which jeopardized public safety.

In both cases, the black community felt the punishment didn't fit the crime; they carried the sense that the justice system had short changed them and would later notoriously get "pay back" by acquitting an obviously guilty O.J. Simpson of murder.

But from my perspective, it wasn't the justice system that failed the black community—it was the media.

Instead of reporting the news as it was, it gave a biased presentation. During the King and Harlins trials, the media shaded LAPD and the Korean community negatively. They did this by glossing over the bad behavior of both King and Harlins.

Because of this, it's easy to see why the jury's verdict caused the outrage it did. How could anyone witness the TV news story and let the guilty parties go? It didn't make sense… unless you were presented with the truth.

The 2020 BLM/Antifa Riots were an attempt to recreate the 1992 L.A. Riots nationwide. This time, the conveniently withheld truth was the overdose of George Floyd. The media refused to correct the viral "I can't breathe" imagery of Derek Chauvin's knee on Floyd's neck. The country was led to believe that Floyd was suffocated by police brutality. The prototype for this vehicle of social unrest was the Rodney King incident, and local prosecutors made sure that the police wouldn't walk free, like the LAPD had so many years previous.

The result of the King trial was that the four officers recorded beating King were acquitted of local criminal charges. Two of the officers were federally indicted and served time in federal prison for about thirty months. I remember when it happened, that everyone seemed to have watched the trial, at least on and off. The names Koon, Powell, Wind, and Briseno became common to overhear.

The trial was everyone's hot topic of conversation. We saw the beating replayed over and over again, so any reason as to why the events from that evening leading up to the beating seemed to pale or be lost to the public. It was almost an overlap between the Latasha Harlins verdict and the Rodney King video without any pause for the city or warning to the Korean community that a spillover effect was in the works and would explode almost a year later.

Why did Rodney King not comply with LAPD's commands when his two passengers did? Or even George Floyd when he was arrested? The decades of excusing or overlooking bad behavior because they're black has had its consequences in not only exacerbating it but also perpetuating it for decades. The same problems I saw as a teenager persist even now as I approach my mid-50s. In turn, it's confirmed my suspicions that treating the problem/system is way more profitable than solving or curing the disease. We pour billions of dollars and legislation into 'trying to solve' racism on a national level, when kids have already figured out it's not racism but asshole-ism that's the culprit. You can find this disease in every race, even Korean.

But at the time… none of that really made its way inside the bubble I lived in with my friends. We didn't care about Latasha or the Korean shopkeeper. We didn't get clued into racial tension—and get angry about them—until we heard Ice Cube's song "Black Korea."

All of us listened to his music and had grown up with his songs since he was part of the rap group N.W.A. (Niggas With Attitude). But "Black Korea" was something else. I still remember Mitch and me listening to the song, looking at each other as we processed insulting lyrics critical of Korean store owners that came with threats to burn our markets down.

Mitch ejected the cassette tape from his car stereo and threw it out the window, saying, "Fuck that guy. Fuck Ice Cube."

We weren't completely in the dark that relations were bad before that song, though. The tension had started to show up in movies, with scenes in black neighborhoods that involved Asian or Korean shopkeepers. Spike Lee's movie *Do the Right Thing*, for instance, had a scene with a Korean shopkeeper swinging a broom to hold off a black group that was rioting and looting. The shopkeeper insists that he's black, too. We laughed at the scene in 1989.

But by 1991, even the relationship between blacks and Koreans was no laughing matter. The depiction of Asians grew more hostile. A film released that year called *Boyz n the Hood* replaced the funny Asian shopkeeper with a store owner described as something like a motherfucker Korean nigga taking money from our community. Two years later, *Menace II Society* featured an Asian liquor store owner being murdered as a plot element of the film.

Looking back now, a cultural clash was inevitable and unavoidable. How could it not be? I had grown up with the music and culture from one group, yet I identified with another, and I saw the two like oil and water.

The politicians and "community leaders" didn't help the situation. They preyed on the anger and frustration from the black community to deflect the shortcomings of their leadership in office, and they race-baited the community to make money. A good example of this is Maxine Waters. She was the congresswoman in 1991, during the L.A. Riots, *and* in 2020, during the BLM/Antifa Riots. Thirty years of her repeating the same bullshit, race-baiting and scapegoating other races, while she, along with her family and friends, enriched themselves.

But though the fueling of poor race relations had been building up for a while, the powder keg didn't truly explode until April 29, 1992.

That was when the jury in Simi Valley delivered their acquittal of the officers who beat Rodney King.

PART TWO: THE RIOTS

CHAPTER EIGHTEEN

The video of Reginald Denny getting pulled out of his truck, hit in the head with a cinderblock, and left in the street splayed out in a pool of blood that aired live on TV was a "what the fuck" moment for many in Los Angeles. I was working that day at the dealership, and the manager turned on the TV news when he heard what was happening. I don't remember if we sold any cars that day, but I do remember that, as we watched the helicopter coverage of the post-verdict protest on Florence and Normandie Avenue, I kept thinking that I used to ride the bus right through that area to get to my parents' market. It was a long ride from Hollywood, an hour and a half to two hours, and I'd sleep on the way through some of L.A.'s roughest neighborhoods. No one bothered me, but then again, I didn't look like the typical "good Asian" kid. And even though I'd sleep, part of me was awake, aware of what was going on around me.

Going home from work that Wednesday, things were still relatively "normal." News reports were coming in about sporadic fires and looting, but everyone in L.A. thought it would be over by that evening. We were all wrong.

The black community was pissed off. The verdict from Latasha Harlins's trial the year before was still a source of simmering anger that contributed to the mood.

"They're killing us!" is what I heard many shout in anger outside the courthouse when the Latasha Harlins verdict was delivered. And now the Rodney King verdict took that anger to another level.

Korean business owners in South L.A. and Compton would be the first to bear the brunt of that anger.

Separated from Koreatown, these businesses were like islands peppered throughout the black community. Korean immigrants found these areas to be convenient places to do business with their limited English skills. However, the cultural gap and friction between business owners and customers was noticeable, and had only grown over the years. There were a few Korean businesses that had integrated themselves with the community—participating in community events, functions, and fundraisers. But the majority just wanted to do business with the community and nothing beyond that. The long hours, strange customs, language, and struggle to survive in a new country kept many from making an effort to connect with their customers or the community at large.

And the added insult, from the black perspective, was when the Korean business owners reached some semblance of success and showed it off by driving expensive cars, like a Mercedes or Cadillac, through the neighborhood streets. To the customers who patronized their businesses, that felt like flaunting and left a bitter taste in their mouths. It was *their* money that paid for those cars.

To those struggling in the hood, it looked like these newly arrived immigrants had stepped on some magical escalator of success, which made rumors of interest-free loans circulating among the black community seem plausible. Never mind that the businesses often employed—unpaid—at least two generations, sometimes three, or that they never seemed to be closed, operating for long hours. And of course unseen was the cramped one-bedroom apartment and the ridiculous methods for the family to "save money!"

There was another issue as well. Back in Korea, shopkeepers and business owners were gregarious and friendly for the most part—but that was not the case with these immigrants. Many were highly educated, with college degrees, yet had to open their businesses in areas where most Americans wouldn't go, even during the day. Many experienced repeated thefts and armed robberies, so they were wary of their customers unless they knew them well. That led to a different demeanor—cold and suspicious—when dealing with the retail public, which added further resentment.

I left home for work at seven that next morning, arriving in Alhambra to start my shift at eight. By noon, the fires of businesses being burned dotted parts of South L.A. and Compton, and were slowly working their way north. My manager knew that to get home I'd have to go through Downtown L.A.—which was experiencing some looting—so he told me to leave work early. But I only had a few hours until my shift was over anyway, and what was I going to do if I got home early? Huddle in front of my TV, gawking at the video footage of the looting and burning? If I was at work, there was at least a chance of making a sale.

There would be no cars sold, because no one was coming in. Everyone in the city, and in the surrounding cities, was doing what I didn't want to do: staying at home, glued to the TV.

My shift ended a little before six p.m. As I drove home, I could see the smoke from several fires south of Downtown L.A. The flames had gained momentum, spreading into areas outside of South L.A. and Compton, and firefighters were no longer making the effort to put them out… because they were being shot at; they required an LAPD escort. Looting occurred as far north as Hollywood, where we got the infamous video of a man stealing a giant TV, then dropping it and pulling out a pistol on a female news reporter with her cameraman. All of it was caught, on camera, outside Circuit City, a giant electronics retailer on Sunset Boulevard, east of Vermont.

After making it home, I changed into my street clothes and drove along Hollywood Boulevard, having learned from the news reports that lootings were occurring there. Being curious, I wanted to see for myself how bad it was compared to the news on TV. There was a corner liquor store on Bronson and Hollywood, and people were going in and coming out with liquor bottles—looted, of course. Someone had broken into Frederick's of Hollywood, a popular women's lingerie retailer, too. That memory stuck with me, because of all the places to loot… Frederick's of Hollywood? I suppose there isn't a better time to pick out sexy lingerie for your significant other or yourself than during social chaos. There were a few others with their doors pried open or glass shattered. Only the stores with steel roll-up doors remained intact and untouched.

I went south on Highland Avenue, then headed back home and turned on the TV. A local news channel became my background noise. All around the country, people were doing the same thing: watching on TV as businesses were looted and/or set on fire, mainly in areas that had a predominantly black population, such as South Central, Compton, and Watts.

The main targets were Korean-owned businesses.

There were, of course, non-Korean-owned businesses affected as well, but the majority of the losses were Korean. From my father and mother, I knew and understood the sweat and stress that came with owning a small business in a neighborhood most wouldn't drive through on a bright and sunny day. The hardest video for me to watch was of a Korean woman witnessing her business burning after it had been looted, and in between sobs saying that what was happening wasn't right.

It wasn't, and I felt my anger grow, wondering how this was all going to play out.

The natural assumption was that the riots would move north, and the black community's rage would soon be felt in Koreatown. In fact, the riots were already spreading, with lootings in Hollywood, Culver City, and other areas in Los Angeles County—and many of these were not because of "social outrage" but out of simple opportunity. There was a total lack of LAPD anywhere, and that emboldened people to participate in the chaos, without consequence.

Around nine, my phone rang. It was Mitch.

It had been a few months since we'd spoken. He'd started work at a large office supply retailer not long before and was picking up as much overtime as was being offered. We worked about half a mile away from each other, yet hardly saw each other.

"Hey, what's up, Mitch?"

"Are you watching what's going on?"

"How can I not? It's all over TV, and you can smell the smoke."

"You know why I called, right?"

I did. Mitch's brother's business was on Vermont Boulevard, between Venice and Washington Boulevards. It was a stereo installation shop that would enhance your vehicle's sound system by installing premium equipment like amplifiers, larger speakers, or speakers all throughout the vehicle to help accelerate your eventual hearing loss. With the way things were going, his shop was at risk.

Mitch knew that if anyone was going to go out during a time like this, it would be me. I'd spent enough time with Mitch and his family to consider him a close friend. I'd eaten food prepared by his mother at his house so many times. His oldest brother was a good guy and never tried to press, intimidate, or make us do dumb things even though he was bigger and had a reputation in the past of having a quick temper. Part of me felt obligated to go because of the hospitality they'd shown me over the years and a sense of duty to a friend.

"Yeah, I know why," I said into the phone. "What about the other guys?"

"No, just us. Those guys aren't Korean. They wouldn't understand. I don't want to ask them."

Then he started going into how this was about us being Korean, which surprised me. Mitch hardly ever brought up the fact that we were Korean (with the exception of making fun of my Korean accent, usually calling it a North Korean accent, even though he's never met a North Korean). In truth, being Korean wasn't something we gave much thought to. We considered ourselves Angelenos (Los Angeles residents), especially given the variety of our friends. Yet we couldn't deny that we'd been singled out as targets in the riots. We were forced to acknowledge our identity—and that we were not the same as everyone else at this time.

"My brother is boarding up because it's getting close to the shop. I want you to go with me."

"All right," I said. "Come get me."

"I'll be there in the morning. The usual time."

Mitch didn't have to try hard to convince me. I just needed a good reason to go with him. Our friendship and wanting to protect his family was enough.

I slept well that night. Sleeping has never been difficult for me, even today.

CHAPTER NINETEEN

I was up at seven, took a shower, dressed, and got my shotgun. It was a Remington 870, a purchase made with my first paycheck at eighteen and still part of my collection. After loading it, I dumped the rest of the shells from the box into a bag, then dumped in a full second box as well.

The familiar sound of Mitch's Toyota Corolla came down the driveway, stopping at my window.

"You ready?"

"Yeah, I'll be out."

I picked up my shotgun and the bag of shells, then opened the bedroom door leading to the dining room, which opened up to the living room. My father was standing in the living room, tucking a revolver under his belt above his right front pocket. It was his Smith & Wesson .38 Special. I remembered finding it hidden in the market at Huntington Park when I was twelve and showing my brother, who was four, and telling him to never touch it, then putting it back on the high shelf as if it had never been found.

Now I locked eyes with my father in the living room. *Damn, what's he going to say?* went through my mind as I prepared to leave through the back door with my shotgun and bag of shells. To this day, I'll never forget the look he had. It was neither reprimanding nor approving—just an acknowledgment that we were both headed out for the same reason.

I think that was the first moment in my life that my father didn't look at me as a boy. It was a look between men, knowing that we were going out for a specific purpose. A serious purpose. I couldn't imagine being like that with my own son—but then, we have a relationship dynamically different from the one I had with my father. My father perhaps trusted his gut instinct regarding my background on the streets, knowing that I was entering an environment I'd left behind not that long ago. And he knew of my familiarity with firearms, having found my cache of pistols and a shotgun hidden in an overhead storage compartment in the apartment carport when I was fifteen.

With everything my father had been through in life, hardly anything rattled him, but I was the exception. I could be a pain in the neck sometimes to say the least; I knew there were times he regretted having me. His life would've been easier if he didn't care so much and did what many men did: drink themselves into a stupor and let me become someone else's problem. Yet through all the issues I brought home, he accepted me and dealt with me, never giving up, telling me I was a smart kid making stupid choices.

He was right about that.

On the rare occasion when we'd have a conversation, I'd ask him what it had been like going to high school in Korea. It was no picnic; he told me he would go to school with a hammer because of the fights. High schools in Korea have their rivalries even today, but it was much worse, much more violent, when he was a kid. Crosstown rivalries in America usually involve shouting mean things at the opposing school, but in South Korea during the late 1950s and early 1960s, it meant fighting with weapons, not much different than a gang fight. There are a lot of Korean drama movies and series that depict this. But things are better now, since many of the kids today are studying almost 24/7 to attend a top-tier university, in order to get hired by one of the *chaebols* (powerful family-owned companies in Korea) that currently run the country.

I wonder if that background experience, the fighting, tempered the way my father dealt with me. Perhaps my joining gangs and fighting was not so different from how he grew up.

My father's journey to the US began when his father, my grandfather, abandoned his wife and his three children for a younger woman while working in Vietnam as an airplane mechanic for the American military. That selfish decision messed up my father and made his ambition to pursue a pharmaceutical career near impossible, since it fell to my father to support the family (his mother and two younger brothers). That, in turn, led him to join the small group of young South Korean men and women laborers sent to West Germany as part of a financial aid package to help rebuild South Korea's economy, allowing him to send money back to my grandmother. That was how he met my mother, and why I was born in the former West Germany. But my father had limited opportunity to become an entrepreneur while laboring in West Germany, and so the idea to immigrate to America took hold of him.

I suppose it was that hard background, along with the years of owning markets in neighborhoods with the possibility of an armed robbery occurring at any moment, especially in the evenings, that made my father almost unshakable. The only time I saw him broken was when my mother passed away.

His first armed robbery was on Christmas Eve in 1979, and I was there. It was near closing time, around nine thirty p.m., and we would close the market by ten. I was out playing with my friend Anthony, who lived across the street from the market. Anthony had a large extended family; his mom was black, and his uncles looked Hispanic. I forget what happened to his father. All his uncles were Marines, and for the holidays, they'd get together at their sister's place with their Marine buddies and have a barbecue, drinking Budweisers starting in the early afternoon. His oldest uncle, his mom's older brother, had a curly beard that matched his dark brown hair. We saw him frequently. He was affable, boisterous, and got along well with my father. He was stationed in Okinawa when he served, and my father was born in Tokyo, so they would often say phrases in Japanese to each other while shaking hands. It wasn't uncommon for my father to get invited to their house during these barbecues. He'd go there after closing up the market and bring a couple of cases of Budweiser with him.

That Christmas Eve, Anthony and I had been playing, and we headed to the market because it was getting late and he wanted to buy some late-night snacks, since we were going to be closed the next day for Christmas. When we owned the markets—the one in Boyle Heights, and after selling that, the one in Huntington Park—the only days off were Christmas Day and Thanksgiving. We worked the rest of the 363 days. The "two-week vacation" was something I knew didn't apply to us. My spring breaks and summer vacations were spent helping at the market, with the exception of my Boys Club camping trip when I was nine.

Anthony walked ahead of me as we entered the market, then quickly turned around and tried to push me back out. But I kept walking, unaware of what he was doing. We walked into a robbery in progress. Two men were standing over my father, who was lying face down on the floor with his hands behind his head. One of the guys had a rifle, and the other was kicking my father, yelling, "Where's the money!"

Anthony and I both turned to walk out, but one of the men called out, "You. Come here."

"I think he's talking to you," whispered Anthony.

Part of me wanted to sarcastically tell him, "I know," but the other part was too terrified to talk at all. So I slowly walked toward the men with my hands up, beginning to cry. They made me lie on my stomach, face down on the floor like my father. Meanwhile Anthony ran back home and told his uncles that the market was being held up at gunpoint.

"Where's the money!" the robber shouted again at my father.

"Only in the register. I don't have any."

"Don't lie to us!"

The one holding the rifle hit my father on the head with the butt of the weapon, creating a gash. Blood started to dampen my father's hair.

"Where is it?" shouted the gunman, this time at me, while keeping the rifle pointed at my father.

"Don't tell him where it is!" my father said in Korean.

I was seven years old and crying while watching my father get beaten, both of us face down on the floor.

"It's there!" I screamed, pointing to the bottom of a cooler that displayed the meats and cheeses. I didn't care about the money; I just wanted these guys to leave. My father kept cash in that cooler, either to replenish the register or just to store anything extra when the register was full.

As soon as I said that, the guy's partner went behind the display case, opened the bottom door, and found the leather pouch with the cash in it.

As he returned to his partner, I'll never forget what I heard and saw. A rumbling noise came from the entrance, and I turned my head. It looked like a living tidal wave of men barreling into the store, cursing and shouting, with Anthony's oldest uncle leading the charge, and the rest of his uncles and Marine buddies storming in, shouting, "YOU MOTHERFUCKERS!"

I don't know what else they said, because by then, they were on top of the two guys. It was surreal. The oldest uncle rushed at the gunman and got his hands on the rifle, wrestling for control, while the other robber was knocked down along with some shelving and became a human punching bag.

The rifle discharged with a deafening bang, and that was when my father realized it was an actual firearm. Until that moment, he'd thought it was a BB gun. He told my relatives that hearing the rifle go off shook his reality, and that was when he felt fear.

For the next several minutes, it was everyone beating the two guys, while my father navigated through the beatdown to recover the leather pouch. I got up and joined the melee by repeatedly kicking the ribs of the guy without the rifle. I'm sure one of the images I left my father with that night was his seven-year-old son kicking a robber with gleeful anger, eliciting occasional groans from the criminal. By the time LAPD arrived, the faces of the two men were badly mashed, eyes swollen shut, with blood dripping off their hair and trickling down the sides of their necks.

My mother was pregnant with my younger brother and went home early that night. I still thank God that she wasn't there that night. She met us at General Hospital, later renamed County USC. The gash on my father's head got bandaged up, and he looked like a World War II Japanese kamikaze pilot, missing only the red circle in the middle of the white bandage on his forehead. Anthony's oldest uncle had messed up his hand from punching the guy's head and face so many times; we all spent Christmas Eve at General Hospital for a good part of the evening.

I eventually went home with my mother. My father went with the uncles to Anthony's place to drink and recount the events of that evening with the rest of the men. He didn't come home that night. He either spent the night at Anthony's or slept in the market.

He returned to us just before noon the next day, Christmas of 1979.

That was my father.

And now, he was going to help protect what our Korean community had built.

CHAPTER TWENTY

"Let's go," I said to Mitch as I closed the car door.

It felt like old times, not when we were skipping school, but hanging with our crew and ready to ride through a rival neighborhood. The air was thick with the smell of smoke, and ashes were still drifting down, carried by the wind, like perverted snowflakes covering everything in black, white, and gray. We took the smaller streets to get to the stereo shop, avoiding large streets like Western or Vermont Avenue, because we didn't want to encounter a bad situation before we arrived at our destination.

"I got this," Mitch said as he showed me his older brother's Beretta 92FS, a nine-millimeter pistol that Mel Gibson popularized in his 1987 film *Lethal Weapon*. It's still a great movie even after almost forty years.

"Do you have a paper bag?" I asked him.

"I'll get it at the shop."

The paper bag, before all the bags went plastic, was to cover the pistol and retain the shell casings while you were shooting. It was a way to keep LAPD from tracing a shooting, by not leaving evidence at the scene. And the LAPD from the 1990s would find you. They had the funding and an ear to what was happening with street politics. During an incident years before, I was being detained for walking with a group. CRASH rode up after being called by a "black and white," or uniform officer, and the CRASH officer rattled out who we might be and what the politics were on the street.

And he was getting it right.

It was a good program; it just needed better guidelines and oversight.

When we arrived at the shop, Mitch's older brother, along with the two other owners and their black and Hispanic employees, were moving the larger equipment away from the windows and getting plywood ready to place over it. We walked through the shop to help, but most of the work was already being handled. We were all armed, including the employees.

Mitch's older brother had a look of concern on his face as he said, "They're coming north. It's getting closer."

Since things were being handled at the shop, he asked us to drive by the plaza on Olympic and New Hampshire Avenue, a small street west of Vermont Avenue. He wanted us to check in on some friends he had there, along with a few business associates.

Mitch and I got in the car and started making our way over. When we pulled up, some of the guys, men in their thirties and forties, were moving their cars to create a barricade to the entrance and a makeshift wall for cover. A green wrought-iron gate was installed after the riots.

An older gentleman, maybe in his fifties, approached us. Mitch relayed in Korean who'd sent us and why we were there. The man told us that a white Toyota Corolla four-door (similar to the car we were in) had been driving by the plaza and taking random shots at them.

We knew who that was; gangs have certain cars they favor. Blacks and Mexicans liked Buicks, Chevys, and Cadillacs. Salvadorans who were MS liked Toyota Corollas.

As we were listening to all this, I couldn't help but think of Carlo. I hadn't spoken to him in over a year, and the only updates I received were from Marty or Ronnie. His new life was bringing turmoil to his family, and I knew from the way Marty and Ronnie talked, the incidents weren't being embellished or exaggerated.

Damn, Carlo, are you riding around with your crew and taking shots at these old guys?

I couldn't wrap my head around that. Carlo and Marty were close; they'd practically grown up together and at times acted like brothers. Carlo even went and helped out at Marty's parents' swap meet stall. They trusted him. Does all that disappear, given enough time and influence? Does the friendship and closeness from the past no longer count for anything if you're with a new crowd? What if Mitch and I were to run into Carlo and his crew? Were we going to have dialogue, or would we start shooting and pretend we didn't know each other? How crazy was Carlo going to get? Also, how high was he going to be, and on what?

I was quiet and didn't say anything as Mitch finished up the conversation. But as we drove away, I shared my concern.

"You know who was shooting at them, right?"

"I know," Mitch said.

"He might be out here, too."

I didn't have to say Carlo's name.

Maybe things would've been different if Marty or Ronnie were with us. Ronnie would've assured us it'd be cool between all of us, while Marty would say that nothing was going to happen. But neither of them were there—we hadn't all parted on the best of terms.

The next moments were quiet. We were scanning the streets and blocks. We were hunting.

Mitch and I didn't ride like this together, but we'd done it with our own guys from the past, so nothing needed to be said. We drove quietly through the smaller streets of Koreatown, crossing the larger avenues, scanning both sides as we drove through the different neighborhoods.

You could tell the territory you were in at any moment from the graffiti on the walls, including the intensity of graffiti battles on the borders. Relying on our knowledge, we navigated specifically in the territory that would serve as our hunting grounds. But given all that was going on, we didn't know who was going to come at us.

"Make a right," I said when we were south of Olympic Boulevard and east of Normandie Avenue. We were on the edge of MS territory and were getting ready to go north again.

As we slowly approached the next intersection, we saw it: a white four-door Toyota Corolla.

"Slow down, Mitch."

It was a matter of time before we caught up to the vehicle. However, the scene was different from what I expected or imagined. The car was parked on the lawn in front of a two-story, multi-unit building on the corner of the block, and three Hispanic guys were washing it. One was shirtless, the second wore a tank top, and the third was in a white T-shirt. The tank top guy was wearing shorts, and the other two were in blue jeans and looked the part of MS members with their short hair and Nikes. They were all laughing and talking.

All that stopped as we slowly approached, staring at them. The change in their mood was like going from day to night.

Is it these guys? I thought. *And why are they washing their car? Where's the fourth guy? Did the older Korean guy count correctly?*

Mitch slowed further, and the three guys froze. They knew we had bad intentions; it was obvious. We were looking at them intently, trying to figure out if these were the guys. The last thing we wanted to do was shoot people who had nothing to do with our situation. But they knew what kind of Koreans we were and recognized us as such immediately.

As we were directly across from them, I lifted my shotgun to display it, though I kept it pointed down at the floorboards. Likewise, Mitch pulled out his pistol, not pointing it at them but just holding it up so they could get a clear view of it. I nodded at them, and in turn, all three nodded back at me. The message was sent and understood, whether it was these guys or not. *Not only are the older guys shooting back, but the younger guys will come hunt for you as well.*

Asian gangs from that era, and even now, have that reputation in Los Angeles.

I don't know how many other younger guys were doing what we were doing, but I know one of them, Eddie Lee, gave his life that week. Eddie was shot by a Korean business owner who mistook him for a Hispanic gang member when he and his friends drove up to a storefront to offer their assistance. Being dressed like a Hispanic gang member didn't help, especially during the evening. Eddie was a member of a gang called CYS, and part of the Koreatown subset referred to as Ktown Crazies. I saw an interview with his parents sometime after the riots, and the sadness in their eyes hit me; I imagined my own father carrying that grief for the rest of his life. It was difficult to think of what life would've been like for my father if I had met the same fate as Eddie that week.

I've seen comments from some of Eddie's friends, posted below a couple of the 1992 L.A. Riot videos on YouTube, saying how much they miss him. For them to do that even after more than thirty years have gone by, he must've been a really good friend.

Mitch and I drove through the rest of that neighborhood, wondering if we'd inadvertently given the guys we were looking for a pass. We stayed near the plaza and went out on patrols in all directions, hoping to run into another white

Corolla. As we drove by the plaza, the older guys raised their hands to acknowledge us, and we reciprocated by doing the same.

Several hours later, we pulled back into the plaza, and the same older gentleman told us they hadn't seen the white Corolla since we'd first arrived. So maybe it was those guys washing the car after all. We went by the same street where we'd last seen them, but they were gone. It probably *was* them. They didn't anticipate two much younger Korean men would drive by unexpectedly, flashing a shotgun and pistol—or the potential that their actions might explode into bigger "street politics" than simple pot shots at the older Korean businessowners.

We could've shot and killed all three of them that day, and given the situation, no one would have suspected it was two Koreans. We were in the same type of car as MS, and their deaths would've been assumed to be due to an inter-gang dispute. We didn't talk about it, but we knew that if we had been wrong about those guys, it would've weighed on us, especially me. I was the shooter. It was my job to finish them if we determined they were the guys.

I suppose God had other plans for me at that moment because my life would've turned out much differently if things had gone in that direction—regardless of whether or not I was caught by LAPD.

Throughout the morning as we drove through Koreatown, the lack of LAPD anywhere was unreal. In the 1990s, LAPD had a daily heavy presence throughout L.A., and you could count on seeing a squad car after several blocks on a normal day. It was such a stark change that anyone with my background couldn't help but notice it immediately, especially with how few cars in general were driving around the city. The news kept repeating about the lack of police presence and that Daryl Gates "pulled them back" but a standdown order was never given. Semantics. Just because it's called something different doesn't make it different. No LAPD.

The day blurred once we had the "ok" from the older guys at the plaza that no one was shooting at them anymore. I never put together "Rooftop/Roof Korean" with the 1992 L.A. Riots because, technically, I wasn't on the roof. The older generation took that iconic position, naturally protecting their livelihood. Simply calling it a "business" impersonalizes what their establishments meant to the people raising a family and building a future in this country.

Thursday was the lootings and fires in the south. Friday was the running gun battles between us and MS along with the rest of L.A.'s gangs. The random shots and succession of not-so-random shots throughout the day became background white noise. As long as the gunfire was heard at a distance, we were fine.

Olympic Boulevard was empty, with only occasional cars intersecting from the smaller streets. We stayed clear of the boulevard as well; It was too large of a street, and it would be easy to get ambushed or tailed by another group out for lawless fun.

It may be surprising to know this, but we were wary of other young Koreans driving around because Mitch and I were not in our "territory." Our neighborhood and "friends" were north of Beverly Boulevard, an unofficial dividing line between the gangs we were associated with. That meant that in addition to possibly running into Carlo or other MS and Hispanic gangs, we would have to contend with fellow Koreans from opposing gangs.

Among the Korean gangs, it's a stretch to say that ethnicity kept everyone on the same side that day. Maybe some of the other guys discussed a temporary truce, but we weren't a part of it if that was the case. We were wild cards thrown in the mix, out on our own for our own purposes.

It would've fallen to me to do the talking if we ran into anyone. I would've identified who I was and discussed a temporary truce as well and shared information as goodwill.

But by keeping to the side streets and maintaining our distance from other traffic, it never came to that. Constant vigilance was our mode of operation. We never drove faster than we could observe and take in, and always with steady precaution because all of Koreatown had become a battleground.

The barrage of gunfire, smoke and lack of sirens felt as if "this was it" from the viewpoint of a pre-Internet teenager. Whatever was happening in L.A., I had a feeling that it was going to continue on and on… with no idea what the rest of the country was going to do. Riding through Koreatown, seeing the plazas blocked off along with watching for anything coming at us was probably the closest I've felt to the "Mad Max" scenario some talk about happening when civilization collapses.

The biggest fear of those defending their livelihoods was arson. Replenishing merchandise that's been stolen on large scale is painful, but the upside is that you still have a storefront to restock; you can be back in business after everything settles. A fire takes everything.

Sure, some business owners had insurance, but anyone who has dealt with providers knows that the time spent waiting to settle with the insurance company is long and arduous. The bills keep coming through it all, unabated.

Mitch and I were usually chatty, but not on those drives. There was a lot going on and we had enough experience to know how things can go from calm to crap in a couple of blinks. The older guys on the rooftops, wielding their rifles in broad daylight and doing their thing around town didn't even elicit a comment. We knew we weren't going to get shot at because we looked distinctly Korean with our haircuts and style of clothing.

The defenders were few and far between, spacing themselves out to best protect the community. Their presence became part of the background, just figures on rooftops. Maybe my father or uncle was among them while Mitch and I drove past them, watching me as I slowly drove beneath them, on the lookout.

There were rumors of markets and other Korean businesses that were protected not only by the owners, but also by black or Hispanic employees and residents because it was the only market nearby for their mothers and grandmothers in the community to buy groceries from. For those working in the stores, their source of income existed only if the establishment remained standing. No one gets paid for showing up to work at a charred husk unless you're part of the cleanup crew.

I don't feel that these stories of the non-Korean neighborhoods coming together to protect the Korean businesses are known or shared enough. Had I not see it for myself with Mitch's older brother's stereo shop, I might not have believed it. The racial tensions felt too insurmountable at the time. A shared livelihood caused people to cross their ethnic lines and exhibit a willingness to sacrifice their own safety. To me, these men are no less a Roof/Rooftop Korean than me and the old guys made famous by those harrowing photographs that we've all come to know.

The day stretched into the early afternoon, and we decided to go west and make our way to Marty's parents' swap meet. The swap meet was surrounded by a tall, black wrought-iron fence with a gate on rollers. Marty was there, working alongside three men loading their individual cars with merchandise.

"What's up, Marty?" I said as we drove into the parking lot.

"Hey, what's up?" He didn't stop what he was doing, just kept loading boxes and other items onto his truck.

He was clearly busy, so we didn't get out of the car. This wasn't a "Hey, it's been a long time, how have you been" moment for us. We updated him on the white Corolla carload of guys, the shootings at the plaza, and finally, MS. Everything without mentioning Carlo.

He quickly said, “He’s not shooting at them.” Even without naming Carlo, both of us knew who he was referring to.

“How do you know?” Mitch asked.

“I know. C’mon, man, he knows me, he’s been here with my parents. He’s not out there. I’m sure he’s out but not riding against those guys. He’s probably riding against 18th Street, but those guys shooting at the guys in the plaza are MS, probably not his clique.”

MS was a large gang with subsets within itself.

It felt good to hear him say that, but I’d needed to hear it from someone who was closer to him.

“But yeah, there’s been carloads of guys driving around from different groups,” Marty added. “But they haven’t come at us.”

The L.A. gangs were definitely out and about. I didn’t know it at that time, but I found out later that scores were settled that week between a lot of them. If there was ever a week where you could literally get away with anything, it was that week. No LAPD presence meant anything was possible—it truly was a gangster’s paradise.

“How’s your mom and dad? Are they all right? What about your brother?” I asked. It’s customary and polite in Korean culture to ask about the well-being of your friend’s family members.

“They’re all inside packing and getting everything to the house.” Marty then asked Mitch about his older brother’s shop.

“Same,” Mitch said. “Moving stuff inside and boarding up the windows.”

“And you guys? Hunting?”

“Yeah. We’ll try and swing by your pad later.”

We drove off. We didn’t go by his pad later, but we knew that Marty would be all right. This was the same guy who stopped traffic during the middle of the day on the 110 freeway to cuss out his cheating girlfriend by jumping on the hood of a car like a man possessed.

Nothing frightened him… or stopped him when he was pissed beyond belief.

CHAPTER TWENTY-ONE

"Hey, you guys didn't eat, huh? We ordered food, so you guys can go pick it up." Mitch's older brother was right, but we didn't have much of an appetite. Whatever appetite we might've had was subdued by a mix of adrenaline and cigarettes—I was a chain smoker when I was younger, and cigarettes were fairly inexpensive back then.

We left for the food. The restaurant was on the west side of Koreatown close to Western Avenue on 8th Street, upstairs in a plaza. Most of the shops downstairs were closed, and the cars formed a barrier around the parking lot. A few men stood guard and granted us access as we pulled up. Mitch took his pistol and tucked it under his waistband, covering it with his shirt. I left the shotgun in the car; Mitch passed me the keys so that if things got hot, I could go and get the weapon.

Inside the restaurant, things looked like a normal day. The place was full, with families and groups of men seated at tables, and a few like us waiting to pick up their order. There was a notable difference from business as usual, however—all the men were shoulder-holstering pistols. Seeing this struck me with pride. It was the first time I felt a Korean identity. I knew that all the men present weren't going to accept the chaos outside willingly. We were all going to fight.

Mitch clearly didn't think about it too much, because his comment was, "Whoa, that's a lot of guns. Oh, this place has the best jajangmyeon, no lie. I had it with my brother last time and his boss ordered it and…"

That was Mitch. He'd sometimes get nervous and start talking without stopping if something was too emotionally heavy.

I knew the Korean community would never be the same. But in my youth and naivete, it was beyond my comprehension that the actions we took that week would reverberate for decades after. That we would send a message to everyone in L.A. and beyond.

Something to know is that it wasn't everyone—the majority of people didn't fight back. But a very small minority can be different. They have a willingness to stand in the face of danger, and against odds that appear daunting, if that's what it takes to protect themselves, their friends, their neighbors, and their livelihood. Others don't understand. They view this as foolhardy, and will shake their heads, not understanding why this small minority is doing what it's doing.

I witnessed the same thing in 2021 with the pushback against the mandates and draconian actions from COVID. That wasn't a Korean-only resistance, but it was just a small minority that fought back, willing to accept the consequences in support of their beliefs and principles.

Mitch was right, though: the jajangmyeon (a black bean sauce with noodles) was really good. Maybe it was the momentous events of the day that heightened my senses, but I've yet to eat the same dish anywhere that tasted as good as the one from that restaurant, which unfortunately is no longer there.

When we returned with the food, everyone sat wherever they could and ate. Koreans, blacks, and Hispanics, all talking, eating, even joking at times. Sprinkled in the conversation was the serious topic of who was going to be where when the sun set; there was a lot of speculation about what the night might bring.

I was expecting to stay, but Mitch's older brother said we had done enough and insisted that we go home.

When Mitch dropped me off at home, he asked, "Tomorrow?"

"Yeah."

He called me later that night, though with second thoughts. “I think it’s going to die down now.”

“Yeah, I saw the news about the National Guard.” The news reports said they would be deployed over the weekend. “We still going out tomorrow?”

“Nah, I think it’s over.”

“Yeah, me too.”

After the phone call, I went to sleep, a lot earlier than usual. I didn’t hear my father return home, but my brother told me the next morning that he came home after I went to bed. We never talked about that week, and I don’t know his story, but I was glad he got home that night.

The next morning, I could still smell the smoke lingering in the air, but it was nowhere as heavy as it had been the previous two days. Since Mitch wasn’t picking me up, I decided to go out myself. The streets were quiet, and wherever I saw the National Guard posted at an intersection, I avoided driving toward them by either turning right or left. In that way, I slowly meandered from Hollywood to Koreatown. With nothing else much left to do or see, and National Guardsmen posted throughout the city, I made my way back home.

The presence of the National Guard was somewhat reassuring, but it felt flat and underwhelming since we’d already done the heavy lifting, and they were there for appearances more than anything else. About a month or two later, I found out that they didn't even have ammo for their rifles and were posted at intersections with empty magazines. The irony of displaying empty rifles after all the shootings, with the community doing the protecting, struck me as comedic. The National Guard arriving on a battleground without ammunition is how I'll remember the incompetence and lack of preparedness of the city leadership and logistical planners of that era.

There was a protest in Koreatown that Sunday and I went. It was my first protest, and I wasn't expecting a large turnout, since there hadn't been that many of us out there defending, certainly not when compared to the total number of Koreans in Koreatown. Yet the people present easily filled the street and several blocks that Sunday. I suppose after the previous several days, the Korean community had enough, and everyone wanted to express it. Those unwilling to stand armed on the rooftops were at least willing to march in the streets.

Eddie Lee's family took the lead of the march, holding his portrait for all to see, as we made our way from one block to the next. The protest took us through Koreatown, with news media covering the aftermath.

The days and weeks that followed were filled with calls from the black and Korean communities to reconcile and find common ground. These efforts were spearheaded by the Christians in both communities. There were talks about developing a better understanding of the cultural differences to prevent what had happened from occurring ever again. I didn't pay much attention to all that, since my fight that week wasn't even with the black community. I didn't hold a grudge against those who were shooting at us either. It was pointless.

MS didn't care. For them, it was a "fun" week of drive-by shootings without consequence, and nothing personal. It's not like a green light order to kill was given by the leaders of MS against Korean businesses in Koreatown; this was done on an individual basis.

I'm confident that they rode out against their rivals, 18th Street, that week, and vice versa. The viral video of David Joo and Richard Park shooting at "the *cholos* and gangbangers" may have involved 18th Street members, but I'm inclined to think it was MS, based upon the descriptions I heard. The common misconception today is that we were shooting at "looters," when in reality, Korean business owners were embroiled in a gang battle, something their younger counterparts that rode out that day were very familiar with.

The rioting, looting, and arson in South Central and Compton were different from the running gun battles in Koreatown. Two different groups came at the Korean community during the 1992 L.A. Riots: the black community and MS13. Perhaps 18th Street was involved on Western Avenue, but on Vermont Avenue, it was MS13. And if you look at it technically, there were three groups in the riots: The black community, the Hispanic gangs, and the individuals who simply saw an opportunity to take advantage of the mayhem throughout Los Angeles County.

The defenders were fortunate that the shopping plaza on Western, between 8th and 9th Streets, had a gun shop. Out of necessity, firearms were handed out to anyone who came to protect the plaza, and when the riots came to an end that weekend, the same firearms were returned to the gun shop. I wasn't aware of that until I ran into the son of one of my father's friends about a week later. He lived two blocks from the plaza and confirmed that firearms were lent out with the promise that they would be returned when everything reverted back to normal.

I later saw a video of an LAPD officer chastising Korean business owners for being armed in public, and possibly asking about the legal registration of the firearms. Ridiculous.

A couple of years later, Carlo was deported to El Salvador. He was part of a deportation program that sent MS members back to their home countries. Inadvertently, the deportations caused MS to spread to El Salvador and to other neighboring

Latin American countries during the 1990s, making them the most notable export from L.A. to El Salvador. Strangely, I became aware of Carlo's deportation only when I was channel surfing and came across a news show, either *60 Minutes* or *20/20*, about MS, and he was being interviewed. I watched in disbelief.

More recently, Carlo was in a documentary series titled *Gangland*. The first episode was on MS. He still appeared to me as the same soft-spoken, introspective, and thoughtful guy. Still the same Carlo. But I know that time and experience have changed both of us.

When I showed my son Carlo's interview on YouTube, he was incredulous over how much screen time my old friend had gotten. He thought it would be a quick camera shot, not a lengthy interview. If anyone could best articulate life within MS during those early years, it was Carlo. He was looking good and I was glad to know that he was still alive. If you've found the video, I'm sure you'll know who he is and his real name.

How could I have ever predicted or foreseen that thirty-three years later, I would write a book about that week, and about the personal connection I had with MS through a childhood friend, a friend whose circumstances had placed us on opposing sides that week? We weren't the typical Asian boys portrayed in mass media—the bookworm nerd or "good kid" on his way to becoming the quintessential doctor or a lawyer. No, we were the rebellious ones. Many of us were from a world where violence was a second language communicated in an instant. Some of us revisited that life for a brief period of time, doing what most could not. As Rudyard Kipling is often credited with saying: "People sleep peaceably in their beds at night because rough men stand ready to do violence on their behalf."

We were those "rough men."

PART THREE: A LIFE CHANGED

CHAPTER TWENTY-TWO

After the Wi Spa incident in 2021 that I mentioned in the Introduction, I arrived home to multiple text messages asking if I was all right. That puzzled me. Why wouldn't I be? Little did I know that the video of me swinging the water bottle was spreading online, and rumors were spreading with it that I had been arrested. There were even calls for crowdfunding to pay for my bail. (Thank you, everyone, for being ready to step up during that time.)

It turned out, the edited video posted by the "journalists" who were too stupefied to physically intervene—which was a good choice on their part—was going viral. The ending, with LAPD escorting me away, was the last thing everyone saw. But in reality, the police weren't arresting me. They just escorted me "someplace away from the crowd," as the officer worded it.

"What about my water bottle?" I asked, and a Hispanic officer replied, "Shit, that was awesome! Don't worry about it, bro. I'll buy you a new one."

But prior to what everyone saw on video, there was another incident that occurred… and this one was far more impactful.

On the opposite side of a green wrought-iron fence, just an instant before I turned to confront the "journalists," I saw a group of about fifteen young men, in their late teens or early twenties, running toward me. As they approached, there was a change in the air around me, almost as if time were working differently, and this unseen energy was making the physical realm appear pliable. There was something strange about the way these men ran. It looked coordinated, like an undulating snake or a school of fish, and it wasn't natural.

The group stopped in front of me, and the guy at the front, apparently their leader, fixed me with his gaze. His pupils were dark, almost black, and his face wore a primal look almost like some sort of beast. His friends, instead of facing off against me at the fence, which is what usually happens, were looking about and not showing much interest in me, like different heads of a hydra.

I should note here that I am a follower of Christ. My walk, and my acceptance of His grace, came after a long and windy road of exploring Buddhism and Islam. I even dabbled in the occult. I had only one spiritual encounter—hearing my friend's mom's voice call out to him while we were reading in his room after returning from her funeral—nothing that was demonic. Spooky, yes; demonic, no.

Until now.

When the leader spoke, his voice was low and guttural, as if speaking was difficult and growling was more natural. "Why are you here?" he asked. He wasn't on drugs; there was a clarity in his tone.

The question stunned me. I was expecting an expletive or the usual posturing that hinted I was about to get a beatdown. And as I was considering my answer, I was interrupted by another voice (a normal one) behind me, asking:

"Why are you wearing a Roof Korean T-shirt?"

"Don't you know that's racist?" added his buddy, and that's where the video picks up and shows the encounter that the world has now seen.

Given what happened afterward, the question "Why are you here?" makes sense in hindsight.

When I arrived in Koreatown and drove toward Wi Spa that day, I instantly saw the crowd in their signature all-black attire —black hoodies, black pants, black mask to cover the face, black sunglasses to hide the eyes. It's a common tactic with Antifa, as it lowers their inhibitions about breaking the law or assaulting someone without criminal consequence. All four corners were occupied by Black Bloc (how Antifa refers to those clothed this way), with about thirty to forty on each corner.

I learned later that many of them were bussed in. While the protest was against having men in the women's sections of the spa, Antifa had arrived in full force as counter-protestors. I am certain it was not a grassroots mobilization by voluntary organizers; there were deep pockets behind the counter-protestors.

Not seeing any of "my people," I knew the protest organized against Wi Spa's policy was not going to have much showing, so I decided to leave. I turned onto Wilshire Boulevard, where I saw an older lady wearing a bright fluorescent yellow shirt with large red letters reading "Jesus Saves." That was when I heard His voice telling me to park and find out why she and three men were talking to LAPD.

I've read about how God "speaks to your heart" or "puts it on your heart," but always thought it was an expression, like a conscience—that inner dialogue or monologue most of us have within ourselves. But this voice wasn't mine; it was His… and it was commanding me. I'd heard it before, but as a soft whisper that left me wondering if it was me or Him. Not this time.

My response was honest. "Do I have to?"

Silence.

I didn't want to. There were a lot of them, and when mob mentality takes hold, it goes in a direction no one controls. Dialogue is limited to emotional slogans and arguments from extremes, to really wind up the other person so they can release that pent-up frustration of not being able to coherently articulate their point until it comes down to "punching a Nazi in the face." But I found an empty parking spot a couple of blocks away and walked back to the woman and three men talking to LAPD.

It turned out they had been assaulted prior to my arrival, when they made their way over to one of the corners of the block and attempted to evangelize to Antifa. They were eager to submit an official report, but the two officers weren't encouraging it, stating they were just there to monitor the crowd.

After failing to get anywhere with LAPD, they said they would return to the crowd that assaulted them and make another attempt to evangelize. I have a lot of respect for street preachers, but in this instance, the preaching needed to be done from behind a wall of other men. In this case, they only had me. I should've walked away, but I felt sorry for the four of them and wanted to make sure they didn't get roughed up too badly. So I followed behind to act as a rearguard, knowing they'd be forced to retreat a second time.

We never made it, because of the counter-protestor from the viral video. I was tagging along with the evangelizers when I saw the Pronoun arguing with a woman holding her puppy. The Pronoun shoved the woman, making her stumble a few steps, and so I stepped up and told it to stop pushing her. It attempted to push *me*, and that was when it got struck the first time with the water bottle. (That's the blow that didn't make the video.) I was backing up as it was coming at me, loud and angry and trying to kick me, when a rotund Black Bloc individual intervened, and the preachers and I found ourselves next to LAPD again. We made our way to the green fence where the video would be taken, and while I was distracted by the demon running up to the green fence, the preachers continued on.

They didn't do so well. The second assault was much worse than the first. This time, one of the preachers got struck on the top of the head with the metal truck of a skateboard, and blood streamed down the side of his head and neck. I wasn't there to see it, but the videos made the rounds on social media.

The guy who assaulted the preacher was later caught when he was spotted at an Anti-Vax/Anti-Mandate rally in Santa Monica in late August trying to spy on attendees. He was easily identifiable because of his particular fat body and his gait; he was even wearing the same T-shirt. Cornered at the train station like a plump rat, he was unmasked and his head was pulled up so the camera could get a clear picture of his face. His picture was shared with other accounts on Discord to archive for the near future. He was later charged with assault for yet another incident and served a two-year probation sentence, which was completed in March or April of 2026.

Within an hour of returning home, Anons—that is, anonymous users of social media—forwarded me the names of the "journalists" in the water bottle video. It took me another hour to look into their backgrounds and join the battle taking place on Twitter (now X after it was purchased by Elon Musk). My account was suspended/banned for a little over a year before it was reinstated in 2023. Anon accounts were sending me videos of other Antifa organizers, and what I'd mentally labeled as their "enforcers," along with their cadre of "journalists" all working in unison to set up, video capture, edit, then spin a narrative or doxx their opposition. I was inundated. And in the days and weeks after Wi Spa, the water bottle video made even more people aware of who I was.

God bless those anonymous accounts. Without them, information and arrests would've taken so much longer.

My Twitter/X account was highlighted on Alex Jones, and a video I posted was used by Fox News to report on the noncompliance with COVID mandates at Tin Horn Flats, a small country western bar & restaurant that became the focal point of resistance against the City of Burbank and the County of Los Angeles Public Health.

Tin Horn Flats was owned and managed by a father, son, and daughter team. The father was overseas, while the son and daughter handled the day-to-day of the establishment. None of them intended to become the center of a political resistance for conservatives and Constitutionalists, but they were getting fined nightly for keeping their restaurant open for outdoor dining. Liberals and Leftists online created a website called "Burbank Bigots," which doxxed anyone supporting Tin Horn Flats, including myself.

As a concerned private citizen, I started putting the players together. I hadn't asked for this introduction to Antifa, but it pulled me in and had me drinking from a fire hydrant of information collected over the years from different protests and rallies—video not only from conservative videographers but from independents and Leftists as well, all publicly available.

In two months, there was enough information to expose the "journalist" from the water bottle video, along with others. Flyers were made with their names, faces, and their tweets or posts calling for violent action. To warn the public of these individuals, the flyers were affixed to telephone poles, utility boxes, and trees, near schools, parks, or anywhere the individuals were likely to frequent. This was done to send a clear message: we know you, and we're united against you.

A side benefit of this operation was that it opened communication between groups that should have connected sooner. Prior to this, innuendo, perhaps a bit of rivalry, and concern with each other being a "Fed" kept everyone side-eyeing each other. But once connected, the network widened, adding connections to contacts within local law enforcement and district attorneys' offices. This group proved instrumental in assisting LAPD with a stabbing by an Antifa member that occurred on August 14, 2021, at the Anti-Vax/Anti-Mandate Rally in Downtown L.A. The Antifa member was identified, even though clothed in all black, thanks to his shoes, a lock of long blond hair that slipped out from the hoodie, his body structure, and gait. Also, because groups of volunteers were patrolling the perimeter of the rally, one group had confronted the individual earlier in the morning as he brandished the knife and accidentally cut himself, making the group laugh at his stupidity.

CHAPTER TWENTY-THREE

I don't watch sports like I did when I was a kid in the 1980s, back when I cheered for the Dodgers, Lakers, and Rams. That was a golden decade for Los Angeles in almost everything from sports to pop culture and entertainment. What I do keep a tab on is global news that deals with finance, economics, and conflict, because of the direct impact it has on our lives, and the clues it gives to the near future. So when I started seeing reports from mainland China news channels that their people were mysteriously dropping unconscious on the streets, it was alarming. And when I saw the fumigation trucks spraying thick white smoke onto the streets and buildings of China, and the terrifying follow-up videos of residents being locked into their apartment units, or even the doors of whole apartment buildings being welded shut—essentially a death sentence—I started getting mentally ready for the possibility that what was happening *there* was going to come *here*.

Of course, it did.

In early January, I purchased N95 masks with replaceable filters, and I was glad I did; by mid-January, they were either out of stock or were selling for four to five times more than what I'd paid for them. In February, I began sending the kids to school (and to their Tae Kwon Do and judo practices) wearing face masks; they were the only ones at this time doing so. In the middle of March, I sat down with the principals of their elementary and junior high schools to let them know I was going to keep the kids at home and have them do their assignments outside of the classroom. It was two weeks after that when *everyone* went into lockdown. Schools, small businesses, even churches were closed. The only places open were the big retailers like Costco, Walmart, and Target.

Initially, it appeared as though these cautionary measures were appropriate. Certainly my imagination went into overdrive when it was reported that a COVID case was diagnosed as early as January from a flight attendant on Korean Air Lines who had a stopover in Los Angeles. I thought of an old movie scene where men in black robes pushed a wheelbarrow, clanged a bell, and called, "Bring out your dead!" It was either that or the apocalyptic movies where bodies wrapped in bedsheets were placed at the end of the driveway.

But all that never happened. We hunkered down at home, with expectations that the world was changing because of a "pandemic" (I put that in quotes because it wasn't that at all), but by mid-April, I became restless and started to ride out with my motorcycle to explore L.A. That was when my perspective on the virus did a complete one-eighty.

I had naturally assumed that the homeless population would be decimated. They had no protections, no shelter, and likely weak immune systems to boot. But no, they shuffled about as always, talking with each other staring out into nothing, smoking glass pipes like it was just another day in L.A. And to them, it was; the only difference was, they had the streets to themselves. It became obvious I had overestimated the lethality of COVID, and the evidence for that conclusion only grew in the months and years that followed.

Nevertheless, by the fall, we were going into full authoritarian mode in L.A. County. Citations were issued for almost all public activity, even lounging on beaches or opening a restaurant to outdoor dining. These draconian measures expanded when L.A. County moved to start implementing vaccine cards, along with talks of required COVID shots for public schoolchildren. I think that was the line for many: their children. People were willing to take the first shot themselves, to retain their employment, and even submit to a second shot and the follow-up boosters. But their children… that was the line that the city and county leadership and unions crossed.

My late friend Mark Perez (who I met at Tin Horn Flats) organized rallies against these policies. He called me to let me know that an extremely large turnout was expected at the next one, and asked if I could help with security.

After the Wi Spa incident, I connected with a local gym owner in Highland Park who opened his gym to anyone who wanted to train. Once word spread, men traveled from as far north as Camarillo, to Long Beach, and Riverside/San Bernardino County. Some were affiliated with conservative groups such as the Proud Boys; others were just friends who banded together to go out and battle Antifa. The best way I can describe it is that we all knew a bigger showdown was coming.

Through the gym owner in Highland Park, I was able to reconnect with an old friend I'd met and trained with years earlier at the UFC gym in Rosemead, California. I'd ride my Honda Shadow motorcycle there at five a.m. to meet "the guys," five of us from five different disciplines: old-school Tae Kwon Do, Shotokan karate, Greco wrestling, Muay Thai, and American wrestling. It was the same routine every day: two-mile warmup run, rotate between weights, calisthenics, battle ropes, etc., then one of us would run a short class of technique in the octagon or bag room. We'd light spar afterwards, but it was more like "touch" with a high level of control. We would open a gym together by January 2022.

I also wanted the peace of mind that my children were trained to defend themselves. They all started in Tae Kwon Do at around four years old, enrolled in judo at seven, and Muay Thai by eight, practicing these three disciplines into their early teen years. I would occasionally add techniques and ideas that got lost or forgotten as combat art was packaged into combat sports for entertainment and profit. During the 2020 COVID lockdowns, I hired a Muay Thai martial artist and professional coach to hold striking mitts for myself and the kids when the gym he was leasing shut down.

The training at the gym in Highland Park was mostly basic grappling and striking. Some people brought newly purchased water bottles as a show of solidarity. This was the group that Mark was asking after when he called me seeking "security."

He was right to be concerned. That rally led to a large street brawl between Antifa and the protestors, on the corner of 1st and Spring Streets, between City Hall and LAPD headquarters. The melee started small, then exploded, with both sides trading blows. The number of combatants on each side was about the same—about twenty-five to thirty.

My goal was to unmask their "enforcers." As soon as one of them was hit and landed on his back, I quickly pulled off his goggles and pulled down his mask. While I enjoyed his quick and panicked reaction—desperately grabbing for his mask to put it back on—I was already unmasking the next black-clothed person closest to me. That person was later identified as a "journalist." This type of "journalist" was part of a larger group of what I view as heavily left-leaning "journalists" who had access to the mainstream media contacts within the *L.A. Times* and NPR to skew the narrative against anyone who opposed the restrictive COVID measures being imposed at that time.

I called for others around me to do the same, unmasking Antifa to take away the strength of their anonymity, and the video of the brawl and my shout—"Unmask them all!"—went viral. Of course, large news media companies such as Al-Jazeera, the *Daily Mail*, and the Huffington Post worded their articles on the incident to shade me and the protestors in a fashion that made us sound like extremists—neglecting to call the counter-protestors what they truly were: modern-day Nazi "brown shirts" acting on behalf of an administration that had turned a blind eye to the violent Leftist language that had inevitably turned into actual violence.

I worked with the LAPD watch commander that day to help separate both sides and allow rally attendees to return to their vehicles without incident, harassment, or fear that from a picture of their vehicle license plate, they would be doxxed. Men young and old, along with different ethnicities—white, black, Hispanic, and Asian—volunteered to escort groups back to parking garages and lots southwest of City Hall. I was recognizable enough by LAPD to help coordinate tactically with their officers to ensure the safety of everyone leaving the event, positioning their officers into a half-moon formation so Antifa was separated to one side.

At future rallies, metal water bottles weren't allowed. In fact, at a rally in November, an officer with the Santa Monica Police Department approached me, addressed me by name, introduced himself, and let me know that my metal water bottle could not be looked at as *only* a water bottle. I drank out of plastic water bottles the rest of that day.

There was an attempt to stop me from attending that rally in Santa Monica by vandalizing my ex-wife's vehicle at three a.m. that morning. Her Toyota Prius was spray-painted with the Antifa symbol (three arrows pointed down and to the left), and all her windows and windshield were smashed. The sidewalk was also spray-painted with the words "Tony Moon is fascist scum."

It was a hot summer night and I fell asleep in the living room. I quickly woke up when I heard the distinct shattering of automobile glass—a familiar sound from my past. The two black-clad masked individuals were about to finalize their damage—the finishing touch was to burn the car by spraying lighter fluid on the roof and then lighting it—but I was already out the door with my Glock, sprinting down the driveway toward them with only the rapid *flap-flap-flap* of my flip-flops to indicate that I was fast approaching. The ominous sound of flapping flip-flops caused those two vandals to drop everything and run.

The police arrived shortly after, and news spread on Twitter/X. Again, anon accounts volunteered information and tips, often relying on chatter from the other side, to help identify the vandals. In fact, some messages I received were from liberal Asians who shared screenshots of chats alluding to the attack and remarks about it after. Overall, I could tell the sentiment was shifting. It's only so long before a lie gets exposed and people start getting indicted… which was what started happening in December 2021. With the help from those anon accounts and some conservative journalists, the San Diego district attorney charged eleven people involved in a January brawl, with many of the eleven having traveled as "counter-protesters" across Los Angeles, Riverside/San Bernardino, and San Diego Counties.

CHAPTER TWENTY-FOUR

I suppose if the 2020 elections were handled differently, and the results supported the actual non-fraudulent count, then you wouldn't be reading any of this, as we'd all exist on a different timeline. There never would've been a January 6th protest in Washington, DC; "@RoofKorean7" would never have existed; and I'd be living my life as I was up to November 2020, with my biggest concern being my kids' next tournament.

My account on Twitter/X was created the day after the election on November 7, 2020, and the anger and pushback would find a focal point at Tin Horn Flats by December. But the event that grabbed the country's attention happened in January.

I didn't want to go to DC for the January 6th protest, but I felt compelled to. The election results were ludicrous. It was difficult for me to believe that not only had half the country voted for that weirdo Biden, but that he'd received more votes than Obama, the first black president. I wanted to join other Americans in adding my body to the overall count of those who showed up in person to protest a fraudulent election. And I wanted to draw attention to the criminal activities that have been videoed and documented—ranging from early morning mystery ballots that move the count higher solely for one candidate, multiple scanning of ballots, suitcases of ballots hidden underneath tables, pizza boxes used to cover the window obstructing the view of poll watchers, and the list goes on. This all needed to be investigated because it was so highly irregular, even when compared to the "hanging chad" debacle in the 2000 election between Bush and Gore.

It was around this time that I heard stories of election fraud coming from South Korea regarding their April election the same year. The 2020 South Korean election had the highest turnout since 1992, with early voting that pushed the liberals into power during COVID.

The videos from the Trump DC rally in October helped make the decision to attend J6 easier. I saw a video of a black woman, with a baby in her stroller and a very young child in tow, being harassed by a rotund white couple for attending the Trump rally. She was asking the couple to back off—her young child was visibly scared—but it wasn't until another gentleman physically shoved the large white woman aside that the mother was able to get away. That was just one of several videos I saw of attendees being harassed or assaulted for merely going to a political rally. It was alarming, so I went to DC with expectations that running street brawls were going to occur at the nation's capital.

It was overcast and cold that morning. I was at the Ellipse with over a million Americans from all over the continental United States. Standing next to the Washington Monument, with the January wind blowing, I saw long lines to the dozens of porta-potties and decided to avoid drinking anything that day. I chatted with everyone around me, and ended up making new friends. Soon small segments of the crowd began to make their way to the Capitol Building before Trump concluded his speech, and as we talked and walked, families with babies in strollers and flags and banners filled the pathway. The mood was festive. Here we were, exercising our right to voice our opinion to the powers that be, asking for a second look at the election results before certification.

I'll never forget J6 and how that day brought so many together. Every type of American was present. I saw the Lebanese flag with its tree, and the Vietnamese yellow flag with three red stripes that I'd often see in Southern California around the city of Westminster, which has a large Vietnamese population. I made a game to find out what state everyone was from—in part as a way to distract from the wind and the cold—as my new friends talked about Washington's stay in Valley Forge and how much colder the Continental Army must've been with their thin 1700s clothing. We spoke of those men with respect and reverence, men we admired for their hardiness and willingness to stay through winter to fight again in the spring.

As we approached the Capitol Building, we were part of a larger crowd, and I noticed a few were directing the crowd with bullhorns. I recognized one of them—the son of a famous Korean reverend known for his eccentricities, like mass marriages of attendees within his congregation.

I recognized him because I saw a documentary of the church, called the Unification Church. They teach a twisted gospel, and in my opinion, it's a cult. In the 1990s, their followers would approach random people in restaurants and bars, dropping a trinket and asking for a donation. For some reason, young Japanese women were the ones to approach us in L.A.

The son had separated from his father's church after he passed away, but he didn't stray too far from cult-like behavior, even fashioning a golden crown that used 5.56 caliber rounds to make the spikes. I couldn't help but think that this guy was a "special type of crazy."

And strangely, I am related to that family. Last names are significant in Korean history, as they denote hierarchy within the class structure prior to the Japanese colonization in the early 1900s. The last name Moon is not common—about half a percent of the South Korean population, so roughly 230,000 out of 52 million.

Moon Ik-jeom, my ancestor, was a scholar and advisor to the Korean royal court. He is a well-known figure in Korean history, having smuggled cotton from China to Korea during the late Goryeo dynasty in 1363. Making cotton widely available for Koreans, especially for the common people surviving through harsh Korean winters with only thin raiment, makes him fondly remembered as a man with a heart for the common people.

Recognizing my distant "cousin" and his encouragement of the crowd to "keep moving forward" made me purposely slow my walk and hold back my new friends. I was getting a weird vibe, so we headed away from that section of the crowd and made our way toward the opposite side of the steps of the Capitol Building. When we arrived, the barriers were getting pushed aside and the crowd was moving up the steps. We found our place at the base of the steps, which allowed us a great view of the whole building, and watched the crowd move up and around as everyone looked for their place.

Throughout the walk, I had noticed that there wasn't any data being uploaded or downloaded on my phone. Others in the crowd voiced the same observation, and assumed it was network overload due to the large number of people. But the camera still worked, and I took panoramic shots to illustrate the size of the crowd. It was easily between one and a half to two million people.

My first indication that something was off was when someone from our group saw an anarchy tattoo (a capital letter 'A' with a circle drawn around it) on a guy's hand. The guy from our group pointed it out to me, and when we turned to face the guy, he must've overheard us because he immediately turned around. I only caught a glimpse of the side of his face before he scurried into the crowd behind us. One of my new friends trailed him, but the guy purposely crisscrossed through the crowd to lose him.

Upon returning and telling us that he'd lost him in the crowd, we started to speculate on why there wasn't any resistance. We had expected a highly visible opposition to our presence, but there was none. Initially, we'd thought that perhaps it was our overwhelming presence that had discouraged them, but finding that individual in the crowd now had us thinking we were infiltrated and didn't know what to expect.

It was difficult to determine what was going to happen next after the barricades were removed on the steps of the Capitol Building and the crowd surged forward. I stood and wondered if the scheduled program with speakers would still proceed. Then we received news from those around us who had a better connection to the network from their friends and family that the program of having Trump and others speak at the Capitol was canceled.

As we all stood wondering what was to come next, Capitol police began making half-hearted attempts to disperse the crowd with tear gas. Maybe the canisters were expired or were from a bad batch, because it was more smoke than gas. Given what I know now, I think it was mainly for show and to skew the narrative as a "violent insurrection."

When the tear gas was launched and there was a need for water for some people at the front of the crowd, I immediately noticed the coordination from a few individuals who seemed to know how to communicate in the same way—either trained or learned through experience—that the Hong Kong protestors communicated during the 2019 Umbrella Movement. Those Hong Kong protestors explained that they communicated through the mass of people, messages passing through the crowd, to get specific items to the front; now I saw that same tactic being used here.

From what I knew about the conservative movement, no one had this type of protest training or experience, and this type of coordination was very different from that used by military or law enforcement, of which there were many former members in the crowd, judging by the lingo I heard. I admired the efficiency with which bottles of water made their way to the front, and at the same time, I felt off about the whole event as the minutes turned into hours.

Much of that time was spent talking to my new friends and neighbors around us. One of them was a woman whose husband worked for the Associated Press (AP) and was told by the AP not to cover the event at the Capitol.

It was much later, toward afternoon, when we heard that shots had been fired inside the Capitol Building. When a friend of mine who was watching the mainstream channels called to let me know that shots were fired, I thought it was just that the tear gas canisters had been mistaken for gunshots. But upon returning to the hotel that evening, I heard that a woman had been shot and killed. The circumstances surrounding that shooting were speculated upon late into the night. It was the next morning that I learned that the shooting occurred inside the Capitol Building, the woman's name was Ashli Babbitt, and she was unarmed.

Hearing that this occurred inside while I was outside weighed heavy on me. It felt like everything went wrong in a very big way.

I was invited to breakfast with a conservative group the following morning and was introduced to the American Freedom Alliance, or AF, an organization based in Los Angeles and headed by Karen Sigmund. God bless Karen for lightening the mood that morning by starting a conversation centered around avocado toast. My thoughts were on the likelihood that the COVID restrictions in L.A. would get even more draconian, and we would be "on our own" for the next four years without any help from the current administration. It was such a familiar feeling.

That morning's plane ride home was the last time I flew without much in the way of restrictions before being placed on the 4S (Secondary Security Screening Selection) by the TSA. Once you're on that list, they painstakingly go through your belongings and do a more thorough search and pat-down—although it wasn't until I flew to Texas in November 2022 that I found out my name was on the 4S list.

The FBI showed up at my door a few months later, in early 2023. I knew they'd show up after receiving notification from

Facebook that Facebook had been cooperating with the FBI since August of 2022. Of course, I didn't receive their email notifying me of that until November. The first question I asked was whether I was being taken to DC. Their answer was an emphatic no. They said they were only there to ask why I went to DC.

When they left, my past experience with law enforcement told me they would be monitoring and watching me. I was right. Not long afterward, they were instrumental in getting social services involved with taking my two kids into foster care for two months until the initial investigation into their "well-being" was completed. That was probably one of the more difficult periods of my life, fighting to have my children returned. Fortunately, they were teens and able to adjust to the sudden change, and weathered it better than I imagined. There were also signs that God sent to reassure us that everything was going to be all right. The most obvious was that they were placed with a solid Christian family with other kids close to their age. The father was a pastor in addition to having a day job.

The J6 investigation finally wrapped up in August 2025, when I was visited and told by two different FBI agents that my case was being closed. This brought to an end the COVID/J6 chapter of my life.

CHAPTER TWENTY-FIVE

Up until November 3, 2020, I was living the "normal" life of raising a young family and going to my children's extracurricular activities, which centered around martial arts. I was the dad driving his kids to and from Tae Kwon Do, judo, and Muay Thai, as well as being on the mat with them sometimes during practice. The week wasn't complete without a weekend tournament, where I would lose my voice from cheering for them and our school. Who I was and what I had done in my youth… that was a long, long time ago. No one would have ever suspected or guessed I was anything other than a father involved in his kids' lives.

But even though my life was "mundane," the quiet whisper and thought of "no one is coming to save you" lingered in the background of my mind at times. I considered the 1992 L.A. Riots a "one-off"—a cultural clash between two groups that spiraled into a free-for-all chaos. I trusted the older adults that were in charge then to address and prevent such things from happening again in the future.

Then came Antifa.

They were dressed in all black, covered from head to toe and carrying homemade shields made from fifty-gallon plastic drum containers with three red arrows pointed diagonally down and left. I wasn't familiar with them until 2016, when they were in the news more and more, especially in Portland and Seattle. They marched on Hollywood Boulevard looking like modern-day stormtroopers clad in all black, identities hidden and intimidating to most. Personally, I found it comical.

These protests were different—highly encouraged by liberal politicians from the start. George Floyd was their new Rodney King, and unlike King, George Floyd wasn't going to say something to help quell the violence and rioting with a "Can't we all just get along?" Instead, the mob would be allowed to foment chaos.

This was also the beginning of donor funding and sponsors exerting control over a riot or "mob." Soon would come reports of Antifa being bused into certain cities to help bolster the protest, video of a white leftist organizer paying blacks to loot, and pallets of bricks conveniently appearing the morning of the protest. It was all to push the American public into accepting a narrative that villainized law enforcement and created negative bias and outright discrimination against white Americans.

The 1992 L.A. Riot was the last organic riot that started and ended with the people. My belief is that virtually every protest that has devolved into a riot since that time has been supported by outside funding or assistance from Marxist organizations such as the Freedom Road Socialist Organization (FRSO), non-governmental organizations (NGOs), trade guilds such as the National Lawyers Guild or NLG, and billionaires like Neville Roy Singham and George Soros. In fact, while writing this book, the Southern Poverty Law Center (SPLC) has been indicted for funding white nationalist groups. As backwards as that sounds, it isn't too crazy to consider—if your organization exists to combat racism and racism is on the decline, your organization will soon cease to exist. The solution for the SPLC, according to the indictment, seems to be to create the racism they vow to defeat.

This logic also applies to homelessness and substance abuse support organizations that hand out clean needles to addicts. If the problem were to truly go away, so would the money.

In my view, the individuals within these groups, along with the financiers, must be indicted with criminal charges along with civil for the damages caused by the mob they financially supported.

My concern for the future turned into a different kind of action—writing—during the 2025 L.A. fires, when emergency services were caught unprepared amid reports of widespread looting in evacuated neighborhoods. The ICE protests the same year in downtown Los Angeles only confirmed that our emergency services (and this is most likely true nationwide, not just in L.A. County) are not prepared for a widespread disruption or direct attack—which again leads me to reiterate that "no one is coming to save you."

You must save *yourself*—and those around you. This means investing in your own defense. This can start with firearms training, but should encompass more as you become proficient. Consider martial arts skills to complement your firearms training, especially a striking and grappling style for the real-life confrontations that won't let you walk away. Develop a practice routine so you can stay consistent.

An excellent book I recommend to all of my students at the gym is *Mastery* by George Leonard. Mr. Leonard was a World War II bomber pilot trainer, and he talks about the different personalities he encountered when he opened an Aikido school with some other students. Without giving away too much, the phrase "enjoy the plateau" is central to the book. Doing this will change your mindset and help you better prepare mentally as well.

Also, join and support your local gun organizations. Two groups I'm affiliated with are the California Rifle and Pistol Association (CRPA) and the Golden State Second Amendment Council (GS2AC). An essential part of responsible gun ownership is knowing what types of legislation are being cooked up to hinder our Second Amendment rights. And that's one amendment we cannot ever let slip away—*none* of the other amendments can be upheld without it. Men much wiser than us knew that criminals don't just come in the street variety; they're sometimes part of our political class.

My advice is to understand that there is a lot of gray within the black-and-white wording of the law. Some restrictions or laws will be challenged in a scenario that's out of the ordinary.

Extraordinary times sometimes create their own unwritten rules. I'd like to close this book by writing down some of what I learned in the L.A. Riots and my experiences before and afterwards when it comes to defending your community.

To win any battle, you must fight as if you are aleady dead.

—Miyamoto Musashi

APPENDIX: A MANUAL FOR HONORARY ROOF KOREANS

PROTECTING AND DEFENDING YOUR COMMUNITY

The 2020 BLM/Antifa Riots—which others may call the George Floyd Riots (named after a criminal who overdosed on fentanyl; a law enforcement officer was scapegoated to appease the country based on a false narrative)—were more about the looting than burning. I saw "Black Owned, Please Don't Loot" or "BLM" signs on store windows, showing support for the organization—obviously to avoid getting their shop looted and damaged. Still, plenty of stores, large and small, felt the effects of the "mostly peaceful protests," which is what they were called by CNN. Interestingly, Los Angeles Koreatown was untouched. Was it because of the memory from the 1992 L.A. Riots?

In 1992, before cell phone technology or the internet, communication was crude. Messaging was relegated to physically going from one place to another to pass a message along. The plaza that Mitch and I went to check on had two-way radios, which were used to cover the perimeter of the plaza, but anyone the next block over might as well have been "on the moon" or even further away. With that in mind, I noticed a few things that were either lacking or not addressed.

Communication and Intel

While having defenders dispersed throughout Koreatown was effective, the lack of communication and sharing of information made the defense much less effective. For example, take that white Corolla that shot at the plaza we visited. Those guys weren't *only* shooting at the plaza; I'm fairly certain they were doing the same to other Korean-owned/occupied plazas in the vicinity.

What if we had been able to get that information to all the defenders within a one-mile radius? With that information, those other locations would have been prepared. Information, and getting it to the right people or group, is the foundation of building a strong defense. If need be, it can even be used as a platform to launch an offensive action.

Set up electronic communication with a backup.

The obvious solution is cell phones. Have everyone that's connected to your group on speed dial or set up so they can be contacted quickly with minimal thumb taps. Also employ two-way radios if you can get them or already have them. It's hard to determine if cell service will exist in your scenario, so having two-way radios is not only a good backup but a better option when communicating quickly and efficiently over short distances.

There are different manufacturers that offer two-way radios. I would consider manufacturers that have recharging capabilities and do not run on AA or AAA batteries. The ones that use the AA or AAA batteries tend to run out of power faster, and the last thing you want is to run out of battery power during a critical moment. If you have an advanced two-way radio that allows you to program frequencies, download a frequency to channel chart to expand your communication options with other radios. Take a weekend to test and learn about your radio. It's one of the most important tools you'll need.

Also, designate a "runner" or "messenger." This may not be as necessary in a suburban setting, but in an urban business scenario, it's one less decision that needs to be made at the moment or "on the fly." You may need two or three "runners," depending on how large of an area you're trying to protect.

The Importance of Video Recording for Later Use

With cell phones, everyone is a videographer now. Attire and vehicle information will help identify someone to local authorities and may reduce the dedicated man-hours before making arrests to days or weeks instead of months. For example: on August 14, 2021, there was a large protest rally against the vaccine mandate and the implementation of a vaccine ID card. Antifa counter-protested the rally, and a brawl started on the southeast-side block between City Hall and LAPD headquarters.

A rally attendee who participated in the brawl on the side of the protestors was stabbed in the chest with a four-inch knife that nicked his heart. (A quick side note: when engaged in a fight, you must have a clear view of your opponent's hands and their placement. The four-inch blade was overlooked during the heat of the melee, and the attendee did not realize he was stabbed until a few minutes later, when he suddenly "felt really weak and off." That was how he described it when I asked him about it later.) Video footage from different angles captured the stabbing and provided enough clues to ID the stabber. He was picked up by LAPD barely two weeks later, thanks to the video.

And it wasn't as though he showed his face. He was clad in all black, wearing a mask and a hooded sweater. But there were still enough clues to give away his identity. One was his gait, which is an easy way to spot someone since it's a very personal movement that's recognizable if studied closely.

Citizen video is powerful, especially after "the dust settles and the smoke clears." That's when the wheels of justice go into high gear.

Drones can also provide video evidence, and in addition can extend the scope of information-gathering. During the L.A. fires in January of 2025, there were accounts of a few drones being seen above some neighborhoods. Some speculated that they might be scouts for Venezuelan gangs who were targeting specific homes and neighborhoods. But defenders can use drones the same way, scouting and gathering video information.

Know Your Adversary

During the 1992 L.A. Riots, Korean business owners faced three different threats: looters, arsonists, and street gangs. The latter two were the more dangerous of the three. Arsonists were intermingled with the looters while the street gangs conducted drive-by shootings at business owners. Prioritize the threat that's developing as the situation spirals out of law enforcement's control.

The 2020 BLM/Antifa Riots did not involve the same type of people as the 1992 L.A. Riots. While there were businesses that were looted and burned, L.A. didn't suffer as much as Kenosha, Wisconsin, where a CNN reporter stood in front of a burning building with the caption "mostly peaceful protest" at the bottom of the screen for the viewers. It was so outrageous that it's now a meme. Many of the rioters and looters were not from the neighborhoods that were being burned and looted, but from middle class and affluent areas to protest in urban neighborhoods that were predominantly poor and black. Despicable.

In the 2025 L.A. fires, the looters were South American gangs taking advantage of fires set by arsonists and the homeless, along with fires started by downed electrical lines, their sparks spread by high winds. These gangs used the evacuation of neighborhoods in the west part of L.A. to loot homes. And they used the L.A. County evacuation alerts to pinpoint where they would go next.

So, know your adversary. Who is making incursions into your shopping plaza or suburb? Are they there as opportunists, motivated politically, or looking for a fight? What is their purpose?

Looters/Arsonists

They're the predictable ones. Looking for an opportunity, they're like human locusts moving from one area/neighborhood to another. Capitalizing on the chaos, they want easy targets. Don't become one. Make sure you have at least four to five men with long rifles controlling all possible entry/exit areas, and they must be highly visible. That will cause most looters and arsonists to move on to an easier target/area.

Gangs and Others Looking For a Fight

These guys are more complicated. People with bad intentions who are armed generally do not want to get into a shootout, unless their emotions are running hot. The gangs shooting at the business owners in the plaza were high on the fact that there wouldn't be any repercussions; they felt as if they could do whatever they wanted. Make those who come at you this way regret that way of thinking. Use height advantages to gain a better vantage point and understand the difference between cover and concealment. Combine both to shoot from angles and places least expected. Kill or maim them. Most importantly, take the fight out of them so they submit to your terms or quit altogether.

Law Enforcement

Law enforcement may or may not be present as the situation is unraveling. At best, they are stretched thin, lacking the necessary manpower to bring the situation under control. At worst, they will abandon an area for the safety of their officers.

This is understandable. During the 1992 L.A. Riots, LAPD was stretched beyond their capabilities, and during the 2020 BLM/Antifa Riots, they suffered outright attacks against them and their vehicles.

During social chaos, law enforcement has now become a target. They're easy to spot, and with enough people, they can be intimidated to retreat or to be rendered non-responsive. The majority of the men and women who serve the communities as law enforcement are what I would call "normal people" who have some training in firearms and making arrests, and have very little in the way of combat skills.

As in other dangerous professions, the patrol officer's goal is to get home at the end of their shift, because each shift is unpredictable. Be nice to them. Now is not the time to become a pseudo-Constitutional attorney and indirectly create another adversary. In 1992, there were some LAPD officers who reprimanded Korean business owners for carrying firearms out in the open, and I've heard there may have been an arrest or two because the firearms weren't legally registered.

You will have idiot cops like this along with those who recognize the necessities of a situation. The conversation should go something like this:

"Hello, Officer, how's it going?"

Here you are trying to greet/acknowledge them first so it sets the tone that you're open to dialogue and not a threat.

> *"Hello, sir/ma'am, I'm sure you're aware of what's going on around your business/neighborhood."*

> *"Yes, we saw it on TV/Internet/social media, and it looks like it's coming toward us. The plaza/business/neighborhood close by has been looted and/or burned, and we're concerned that we may be next. It's the reason why we're outside to keep watch and deter them from coming at our plaza/business/neighborhood."*

The key word here is "deter."

In dealing with law enforcement, designate an older person or someone that the group can agree is levelheaded, even-toned, and who can articulate clearly. Use your own discretion as to how much information you give them. Do not ramble. And stay professional and courteous.

Do not have anyone who has had a negative experience with law enforcement as your unofficial spokesperson. People have varying degrees of reading body language and tone; you do not want any sort of contempt to be communicated.

Then ask the officers, "What's going on with the other businesses/neighborhoods in the area?" If a cop likes you or has a good vibe about you and your group, they may provide invaluable information. Reciprocate their generosity. Let them know that if things get dicey for them, they can come back to your area. Hand them a couple of bottles of water and ask them if they need anything else.

The goal is to let them know that you and your group are *not* part of the problem and get them on their way to deal with the *actual* problem.

Coordinating Your Effort

One of the more difficult things to do during the 1992 L.A. Riots was to coordinate the different groups that were scattered throughout Koreatown. There were more of us defending the community than the eight to ten guys from the pictures everyone has seen on social media. Aside from the other groups that Mitch's older brother sent us to check on, every other group was autonomous, and we passed several driving through Koreatown.

I suppose when Mitch and I arrived at the plaza, if they were under attack, it would've spurred us into action. Logistics was not a strong suit that week, and why should it be? We'd only had a day's notice, and we used what we had learned on our own. The older generation, which was older than Mitch's brother, had gone through South Korea's mandatory military service, while the younger guys had years of street knowledge/experience that were put to use that week.

Everyone's going to have a different background or skill. Try and mesh everything together and let the men group up, but someone will have to lead and make the "final call." Defer to someone who's older or has experience. Remember, this is temporary (hopefully). If it goes longer, then you can collectively decide on leadership roles and committees, et cetera, through a voting process or other means.

Access Control

Controlling potential foot traffic will determine whether you'll be an easy or difficult target. Ease of entry is the first vulnerability that needs to be addressed. If a business is located in a shopping plaza, block all the entry and exit ramps, and if possible, create a wall with vehicles. Work with the other business owners who are present (some may have decided to stay home and hope for the best). If there aren't enough cars to create a barrier, then use individual vehicles to block the entrances to businesses, even if it means parking them on the sidewalk in front of the door.

In a suburban neighborhood, controlling access to your street is straightforward. Put two to three cars at the end of the street, placed perpendicular to the street, to effectively control access to the neighborhood. You may have a person or two who will be annoyed with having to disclose where they live or provide an ID with an address to show they live in the neighborhood. Don't mind these people; these are the clueless individuals who won't understand the situation until they're in the midst of getting looted, shot at, or helplessly watching their home or business burn down. Be firm and stand your ground with these people. Better to hurt their feelings than deal with the violent consequences.

Lookouts

After the entry and exit points are secured, you need lookouts. Post them at high points of the perimeter of buildings, giving them a good view of at least two directions—though a 360-degree view is best. Establish a protocol for identifying vehicles and people. For example: vehicle, color, type, number of occupants, what they're holding, how they're dressed. You can expand on the information as you see fit.

In the beginning, it'll feel clunky, but that's to be expected. You're probably the only one with this manual; it is highly unlikely that your neighbors and fellow business owners have had firsthand experience addressing this type of situation, so be patient and kind. A great majority of people are not accustomed to this level of stress and pressure. After everything is over and order is restored, this experience can be something that bonds and binds your community together.

Deterrence and Mindset

The final step is deterrence and defense. Ideally, this means a visible rifle, though a pistol will work (it just isn't as visible or intimidating). You can even hold a baseball bat or machete as a deterrent. Regardless of what you have, you must be in the right frame of mind, and your energy or "vibe" must make it clear that you're ready to defend your property, family, friends, and self.

I'm reminded of a story from feudal Japan. A samurai was offended by a tea master who wore the garb of a samurai (it had been gifted to him by his lord). Even after the tea master apologized and prostrated himself before the samurai, the samurai challenged him to a duel. The tea master was terrified, but the norms of that period dictated that he could not withdraw from the duel. His lord could not intervene either. Agonizing over what was to come, he approached a samurai friend for advice. After some thought, his friend asked him to prepare him some tea. The tea master, knowing that this would be the last time he would prepare tea for his friend, focused his entire self on the process. Boiling the water, measuring the tea leaves, mixing it, pouring—every step was meticulous and measured, from years of practice.

His friend took a sip, then stated that the tea master must face the samurai with the same focus and ease of movement as he had demonstrated while preparing the tea.

Understanding, the tea master borrowed a sword and set off to meet the samurai. The tea master arrived at the designated point and waited. As the minutes passed, he saw the samurai slowly approaching in the distance. He unsheathed his sword and waited. When the samurai arrived, he placed his hand on his sword, ready to draw and cut down this offending tea master. But then he noticed something different. This was not the same man he had encountered days earlier—the one who had groveled and apologized. No, the look in his eyes spoke of a man who had made peace with his fate and was determined to carry this through to the end. Seeing this, and calculating the weight of the duel, the samurai turned around and walked away.

Logically, the samurai outmatched and outclassed the tea master in swordsmanship, but he did not want the duel in the end. Why? Because the energy of the tea master had changed. Everyone is in tune with energy or "vibe." Body language is unspoken, yet can be read by almost anyone. The odds of losing were high for the tea master, yet the samurai saw no honor or benefit to this fight. The tea master was prepared to lose and die as part of his reality; the samurai was not.

This mindset was succinctly put by James Stockdale, a navy commander who was shot down over North Vietnam in 1965. He was the senior American POW at the infamous "Hanoi Hilton" (the euphemistic name for Hỏa Lò Prison), enduring seven years of torture and isolation. His quote, which became known as the Stockdale Paradox, explains how so many perished while he was able to make it through seven years.

"You must never confuse faith that you will prevail in the end, which you can never afford to lose, with the discipline to confront the most brutal facts of your current reality."

Acknowledgements

If not for my family and the friends I made along the way during the almost 50 years I've lived in L.A., this book would not have been possible.

Thank you, God, for your loving kindness and grace, giving me more time than I deserve to find Jesus and accept Him as my Lord and Savior.

Marcus and Sydney: your generation and future inspired me to write about a past that looked different but felt similar. It gave me the reflection to look at a younger me and remember how the world looked through those youthful eyes; some of those challenges in my youth are not so different from the ones today. Our conversations provided the reminders and lessons from the distant past.

Thank you to my friends "Ronnie, Perry, Mitch, Arnie, and Carlo," for making this story possible. After how we started life, I'm glad we have all lived to see today. Especially you, "Carlo."

Thank you to my Covid/Tinhorn Flats friends. You guys are some of the toughest fighters for the 1st Amendment in America. So glad to have met you and called you friend. Yvette Chambers, Marc Ang, and Casio Shyn: you supported me through one of my more difficult times and helped give me the space in my head to write this book. Al, Michael, Ben, Nick, Claudia, Oscar, Fernando, Toshio and Dilon, thanks for the friendship and Company.

To WarGate: thank you. Your professionalism, dedication and transparency inspired confidence that the book is with the right people. Your patience in explaining things and direct approach made it easier to work together and put this book into someone's hands. Jason and David were great in helping me pull details I would've overlooked. Not to mention Walt's dedication to detail and Nick's guidance on how to best complete the book.

Reader, thank you for picking up this book. Whether you were curious or already knew of the events, I hope to have left you with a sense of clarity and understanding of what it was like in that era. You now have my perspective of the events leading up to the 1992 L.A. Riots—not just for the city, but in my life as well. I hope my story leaves you with a greater understanding of that week, as well as what it was like to grow up in Los Angeles as a young immigrant teenager during that time. Maybe it'll change the way you look at things.

Thank you,
Tony Moon
May, 2026
Los Angeles, CA